Mitchell Walton is 49 years old and is married with three children. He lives near Gosford on the New South Wales Central Coast where he enjoys a quiet life with his wife of 24 years. While he claims not to have many friends in life, the friends he does have are very special to him. Between his friends and family, he believes his life is complete.

My Distant Shadow is Mitchell's first book.

My Distant Shadow

Mitchell Walton

Published in Australia in 2014 by Mitchell Walton
Lisarow NSW 2250

Email: mydistantshadow@gmail.com
Website: www.mydistantshadow.com

© Mitchell Walton 2014
The moral rights of the author have been asserted

All rights reserved. No part of this publication may be reproduced, stored in a retrieval system, or transmitted in any form or by any means, electronic, mechanical, photocopying, recording, or otherwise, without the prior permission of the publisher.

The names of some individual mentioned in this book have been changed to protect their identities.

National Library of Australia Cataloguing-in-Publication:

Walton, Mitchell – author
My distant shadow / by Mitchell Walton.

9780646924847 (paperback)

Walton, Mitchell – Family
Men – Australia – Biography
Man-woman relationships
Love

920.710994

Typesetting and cover design by Epiphany Editing & Publishing
Edited by Epiphany Editing and Publishing
Printed in Australia by InHouse Publishing

To my family and friends, who are totally responsible for me being here today.

PREFACE

This book is a simple look at my life; the life of a complex man who only wants one thing out of life ... to love and to be loved.

Although not dealt with in detail in this book, I suffered at the hands of bullies: both peers and teachers, with little intervention from the people who were supposed to care for me and protect me. This set me up for failure from a very early age.

I made it my mission not to fail in life. However, from the age of twenty, my life has been anything but easy. The journey described in the following pages is one that has turned my life upside down and inside out; with tales of humour, sadness, fun, somewhat dubious behaviour, grief, and, eventually, depression.

I wrote this book in an effort to rid myself of some of my demons, not just in the last twenty-five years, but my whole life. There are encounters within this book that may deeply hurt members of my family; however, sometimes one just has to say, 'This is about me.' It is a somewhat selfish attempt to reconcile who I wanted to be with who I have actually become. There are no lessons to be learned, just experiences to reflect on.

Have I failed? Have I succeeded? I hope you will take the time after reading this book to get in touch to let me know what you think:

mydistantshadow@gmail.com

CONTENTS

Chapter One	Growing Up	3
Chapter Two	The 'One'	33
Chapter Three	My World Comes Crashing Down	49
Chapter Four	Rebuilding My Life	59
Chapter Five	A New Career	73
Chapter Six	A Change of Scenery	77
Chapter Seven	New Love	103
Chapter Eight	Cementing the Relationship	111
Chapter Nine	Meeting the Parents	115
Chapter Ten	Back To Life	121
Chapter Eleven	On the Move Again	127
Chapter Twelve	Life Changing Event	139
Chapter Thirteen	Out Of Character	151
Chapter Fourteen	New Beginnings	155
Chapter Fifteen	On the Lookout Again	181
Chapter Sixteen	Forbidden Fruit	185
Chapter Seventeen	Hot and Bothered	195
Chapter Eighteen	The Fallout	199
Chapter Nineteen	Revelation	207
Postscript		217

CHAPTER ONE

Because I think I'm always right, does that mean that I have to be wrong on occasion just because others disagree with what I have to say? I don't always profess to be right. I just can't remember the last time I was wrong. Is it possible that I can actually always be right? And is there a name that describes people who are always right. Arrogant maybe? Just a thought …

My name is Mitchell. I have a mum and dad, an older sister, an older brother, and a younger sister.

My eldest sister, Darla, and I are estranged and we don't speak. We don't speak because of her refusal to apologise for an unwarranted personal attack on my wife and kids. Attack me all you like, but attack my family at your peril. She has made a point of alienating, not only me, but my wife and my kids. It's a very sad thing to admit that, if your sister died, you wouldn't feel one way or the other about it. It's been that long since I've seen her, I could probably trip over her in the street, apologise, and keep walking without knowing it was her.

My brother, Max, is a successful man, eighteen months older than I, university educated, and generally a nice guy. His wife is an amazing lady. She's funny; almost as funny as me. No really, she is. She's good to poke fun at because she can give as good as she can take. I still think she hooked up with him because of his money, because, really … it's easy to see that I got the looks and the brains. There is only one other thing that she could've wanted (other than the money), but I got that as well. Just so you know Babs … I'm laughing on the inside at the moment. I love ya, babe. They have two glorious kids: a boy and a girl. The kids are very intelligent and very good at sports. Funny really, how they got their good bits from me and the rest from Max. Oh well, can't help bad luck I suppose. I love my brother. He's the son I wanted to be for my mum and dad. I still look to him for approval and it still upsets me when I don't get it.

My younger sister, Sasha, is a very smart cookie indeed. She could have done anything she wanted and probably has. However, her potential, in my opinion, still hasn't been realised. I hope she enters politics someday. I think she could make a real contribution to the Australian community. At the moment, she has an amazing job that most would kill for. She also has two great kids; both intelligent. I can't understand how my nieces and nephews ended up with my brains. Go figure! Her eldest just joined the army to fulfil his lifelong dream of becoming a soldier. Dreams – we all have them, but how many actually come true?

Me – I'm a grown man in his late forties. Over time, I have come to realise that I am different. I mean, I have always known this. However, with recent events culminating in a catastrophic emotional breakdown, I have actually confirmed it. How did I come to this conclusion? For this, I need to go back to my earliest memories as a child. As with everyone, I presume, facts do become clouded when it comes to your own account of how things transpired. Contained within the haze is my own truth.

I am convinced that we are all a product of two different environments. We gain the values that will guide us for the rest of our lives from our families; not just our parents, but our siblings, aunts, uncles, grandparents, and even carers. They don't need to be biological relatives as it is proven that there is no correlation between the values inherited by a child from their biological parents and those of an adoptive parent. Values are learned, not passed down through your genes. The other part of us can either come into conflict with those values or complement them.

To this day, the values I learned from my parents have had an impact on my everyday life. But so have the values I learned from my friends and, in my case, they are frequently in conflict. I often refer to a saying I learned from a man I went to school with: 'My life is a box full of dirt'. This fellow would have no idea that I have been analysing that statement since he uttered it after an exam in 1984. Has my life been a box full of dirt or something else? I still don't know the answer myself. All I know is that I have made a bit of a meal of my life; sometimes with my own help and at other times with the help of others.

My earliest memories start when I was about six years old and living in Padstow – an inner western suburb of Sydney. From that age, I realised that, for me, popularity had a price. I didn't care who liked me; I just wanted to be liked. I was a shy young fella and shy kids didn't get to hang out with the popular trendy kids. Even at such a young age, being out there and being articulate and confident allowed acceptance into the upper echelons of the primary school cliques. If you were shy or not confident in your own skin, you were not allowed in. No way! Kids can be so cruel and tactless. Many of your 'peers' would cut you down as soon as look at you if you dared to try and join their group. You had to regress down to the next level until you found your social standing within the school community. This made it difficult for the kids who were intelligent but quirky-looking or those from different ethnic backgrounds, for they would 'dumb down' so that they could be friends with us 'underlings'.

What did allow you access to a level of acceptance was currency. It didn't have to be money; it just had to have value. At Padstow Heights Public School it was marbles. My brother and I had a skill-set that was second to none when it came to the game of marbles. I still remember starting out with a couple of packets of marbles, which Mum bought me from the shops so that I could play at school. Within weeks, those two small bags of marbles had grown to fill a canvas bank bag. Everybody would want to play me because I had already won all of the most wanted marbles off everybody else. The other kids would be trading all sorts of things for my collectible marbles. It didn't raise the level of my elitism within the social network of the school; nevertheless, I was popular within the marble-playing community.

At the other end of the spectrum, I was also one of the kids who got picked on a lot. I remember I used to hate the Easter Bonnet Parade each year. Everyone's mums had to make them Easter bonnets so they could go in the parade. Most parents would make an effort and go all out. I'm sure that they didn't only want to make little Johnny or little Sally look great, but that there was a competitive streak for the parents as well. Those parents who were too lazy relegated their kids to the back of the parade, where they were forced to wear a tinfoil bottle cap on their heads. I was one of those kids. This was a huge source of embarrassment. It was the type of humiliation that, as a kid, you suffered for weeks after the event. Kids are cruel and they never let you forget. It didn't really matter for the parents, because only those parents who cared enough to ensure that their kids were spared the torment turned up to watch. 'Out of sight, out of mind' for the others.

* * * *

It wasn't long after this humiliation that my parents announced that we were moving to Taree. I was devastated to be leaving my two best mates, Andrew Berkeley and John McDermott. One thing I do know for sure, people are important to me. I usually assess within the first thirty seconds of meeting someone whether they are 'friend-worthy', or not. I'm going to start off telling you about my best mate.

Everyone has a best mate: a mate who sticks with you through thick and thin. Mine is a bloke called Brant. Everyone used to call him Paffy. When I was nine years old, my dad uprooted the family to move from Padstow to Taree, a medium-sized country town of around 32,000 people. I was devastated at the thought of losing my friends, as most kids are when they experience the trauma of moving house. Having said that, the actual move was quite exciting; the promise of living on a farm with my own horse, with cows, and chickens. What kid wouldn't think that was going to be great fun? That was my first experience of knowing that it is ok to lie.

We arrived in Taree – no farm, but a small house in Chatham: a small weatherboard house on a corner. There was no horse, just a dog named Rantoura. The name was apparently chosen by my brother. It meant 'mythical monster' in some aboriginal dialect. Not much different to the house we left in Padstow, except there was no pool and no friends.

The biggest culture shock I remember was the TV. Every night, after the local news, Ted Hebblewhite came on with the stock report as well as the price of wheat and other commodities. Plus ads about the upcoming machinery expo, Agquip, at Gunnadah. Not what I was used to at all. To me, milk came from a bottle, meat came from the butcher shop and all the tea came from China. I don't think it was expensive though because mum would never swap anything or do anything for it. 'Not for all the tea in China' she used to say when asked to do something. And combine harvesters – well, what the hell were they? After a while I found out. Ted told me; I was only nine. I didn't know much about anything at that stage. I just knew that a new chapter in my life was about to start.

I wasn't happy about where I was. As a bribe, Dad used to let me drive the car into the shed when he got home from work. One day, I was with Mum and we'd just arrived home from shopping. I asked if I could drive the car into the garage. After a little nagging, she relented. I got behind the wheel and started to drive in. Mum said, 'That's enough ... that's enough, Mitchell' at which point she went to put her foot on the brake but hit the accelerator. The car did a burnout and created a new opening in the back of the garage, destroying my sister's wardrobe in the process. Mum cried until Dad got home but he actually saw the funny side of it. Ours was a bit of a Jeckel and Hyde relationship. One day, he'd take me out the back and practice cricket with me, the next, he'd take me into my room and belt me for something I did wrong.

Parents are sometimes their own worst enemies. How easy is it for kids to work out that if they complain enough, more often than not you get what you want. That's how I learned to manipulate any given situation with my parents. Sometimes it worked, other times I got sent to my room and had to wait until Dad got home to 'cop a belting'. It was weird because Mum used to be the one to send me to my room, and then Dad used to come home and give it to me. Then Mum would sneak some ice-cream to me so she'd been seen as the 'good one'.

We didn't have much of a settling-in period and so, soon after we had arrived, my dad took me to the local school, Chatham Primary School. I was in that understandable position of being scared; scared of a new place, scared of new teachers, and scared that I wasn't going to make new friends.

As Dad walked me through the school gate for the first time, it happened to be lunchtime. We hadn't made it ten metres through the gate, when a boy just like me came up to us and asked, 'Can I help you, Sir?' directed at Dad.

Dad asked to be taken to the office, which this boy did. At the office, Dad went through the formalities with the principal and then this boy introduced himself.

'My name's Brant. What's yours?'

I said, 'Mitch.'

'We're training for the athletics carnival coming up,' he said. 'Everyone says I run like a horse 'cos I'm fast. I've gotta go. I'll see you around.' And, just like that, he was gone. He was fast!

It just so happened that, when the principal took me to my class, it was the same one that Brant was in. We became instant friends and have been for forty years.

Brant was like me in some ways – an average Joe but a little smarter. But what if he hadn't greeted us that day? What if it was the school captain: a scholar who hung out with a different group of people than Brant? What if it was a person at the other end of the academic spectrum? The fact is that I attached myself to the first person who showed any interest in me as we walked through the gate. Either way, it was a good choice.

I have always wondered if, despite the values I had been brought up with, would my life had turned out any differently had I chosen to hang out with a different group of people right from the start? What if I had thought, *I don't want to hang around with Paffy. He's a weird-looking guy*? Which, incidentally, he was, – tall, slim, haircut like he had a watermelon cut out, painted black, and shoved over his head. What if I had hung out with the school bullies? Would I have become a bully? I suspect so, but who knows? It is only if we subscribe to the 'parallel universe' theory that we can comprehend an alternative to the life we have.

After the move to Taree, I signed up for the Chatham Public School Rugby League side. I was installed into the wing position. I also signed up to play for Chatham Cundle for weekend league. I excelled in both, gaining representative selection in both arenas. I also played school softball and participated in cross-country running, as well as swimming.

I was named joint senior boys swimming champion with Derwood Wickham. He won a couple of races. I didn't win one but I entered everything and got a lot of seconds and thirds. Nobody was more surprised than me when my name was called out to collect my trophy with Derwood.

When we went to inter-school league carnivals, it wasn't unusual for me, not just to be the highest try scorer for our team, but for the whole carnival. That wasn't enough though. It was ok to score tries; however, when the game was over I was no longer part of the team. I was always a bit of a loner.

One game I remember, we were winning. I dropped two balls in a row. I didn't receive another ball for the rest of the first half and I was taken off for the second half. My grandfather had travelled all the way from Sydney to Port Macquarie to see me play. He only saw me play for ten minutes. I was embarrassed, not for dropping the ball but for being left out of the rest of the carnival by the coach.

As I was one of the youngest players in the side, my shyness was apparent to the older guys and, as a result, this was seen as weakness. The ridicule, torment, and bullying I suffered was nothing short of soul-destroying. My own teammates were spitting in my hair and in my face and forcing my face into dog shit, and Dennis, the coach, didn't care enough to stop it. I lasted two seasons. It was a shame, because I was good at rugby league; better than at anything else I did. I loved it. I used to think that mum and dad didn't really care about me. They knew I loved to play footy, but they never asked why I quit. I thought that was odd.

* * * *

Dad decided to buy me a small sailing boat: a Sabot. I wasn't keen on water after seeing 'Jaws' at the drive-in but I decided to give it a go. I didn't mind the concept of sailing but this was one sport I was shit at. I could get from 'A' to 'B' ok but not very fast. As it turned out, not very dry either. My first ever outing in my Sabot was with another fella my age who, incidentally, was far more experienced than I. We ended up getting rescued from the 'drink' three or four times. Each time we capsized, I wasn't at all interested in righting the boat. I just couldn't get on top of the overturned hull quick enough. I didn't want to become shark food. You know ... 'Jaws'.

As the season progressed, so did my captaining skills. I was getting really good at this sailing thing. It got to the point where I was coming last, but we were dry by the end of the race. I was that happy to finish a race without having to be rescued ... outstanding!

Now that I was proficient in Sabots, I decided that I would move into VJs (Vaucluse Junior). They were a sailing skiff that had a sealed cavity for buoyancy so they wouldn't fill up with water when you capsized. That was my kind of boat. Chris Cusford and I used to sail together and, again, we were slow. I can't remember why, but one day I got the shits with Chris for having a go at me. He fell overboard so I just sailed off without him. It was his boat, which made it all the more funny – to me anyway. The crew in the rescue boat 'politely' advised me to come about and go and pick him up. I reluctantly did so. Chris and I never sailed together again. And that was the end of my illustrious sailing career. Go figure!

* * * *

In primary school, I hadn't yet experienced a school social: a dance on a Friday night. Who'd have thought that kids would want to go to school out of school hours? Anyway, it was there that I developed my first crush. This was on a girl named Sue Hawkins – a tall, slender girl with long, blonde hair. Very attractive! Over time we ended up 'going' with each other. We were only ten or eleven years old.

It wasn't long before I found out that Sue did ballroom dancing on a Tuesday night at the sailing club. Even at such a young age, I thought this was a great opportunity to cement our relationship; you know, by doing something that she liked to do. I didn't tell my mum and dad why I wanted to do it but they thought it was a good skill to have. What I didn't know at the time was that I would spend a little time at the beginning of the night talking to Sue, then about two per cent of the time dancing with her. The rest of the night would be spent dancing with all the oldies who were also there to hook up. Doesn't sound too bad; however, for an eleven-year-old boy, there's nothing worse than getting pulled in close and personal to an old lady who smells of naphthalene. It just wasn't worth the little time I got to spend with Sue. I may as well have opened my chest of drawers at home and hugged jumpers all night. That's what it smelled like. Anyway, the dancing didn't last long so I had to resort to plan 'B'. All I had to do was think of one.

I used to ride up and down Sue's street so that she'd notice me and come outside. We'd go over to the park and hop on the swings and talk about kid's stuff. It wasn't kid's stuff at the time though. We were solving the problems of the world. You know, all the important things like who else liked who and who was getting dropped.

The demise of our relationship finally happened when I became jealous of Sue talking to other boys. She couldn't not talk to them. She was very popular but she couldn't handle me questioning her about them. She came up to me one day outside the toilets and said, 'Mitch, I like you but I can't go out with you anymore'. In hindsight, that was a very brave thing for her to do. In those days, at that age, a girl usually got one of her friends to tell one of your friends that you were dropped, then that was it. Everyone was happy again and you moved on. We were still friends though, and that was cool.

It was fate that, one day, I was riding my bike with Sue up and down her street when I saw a friend who was on his way to hockey training in the park across the road from Sue's house. I sat down on a log and watched. They were coached by a man by the name of Roscoe Latrobe. He kept looking over at me and asked if I would like to try out. I thought it looked like fun so I had a go. I tried out as a goalie because they didn't have one. After that first training session, the coach asked if I wanted to play. That was when I went from a team that abused me to a team that appreciated me.

We didn't set the world on fire that year but I received the 'Most Improved' trophy for the year. After that, I went from strength to strength, gaining representative selection in both school and weekend arenas. I turned down the position for the Colts side because it would've meant that I had to leave my club side and play for the Colts full-time. I wasn't about to leave a club that had given me a second chance.

Never once in the seven years I played hockey in the Manning Valley was I made to feel insecure or worthless. That dubious honour was left to my football coach, my teachers, and, to a lesser extent, my parents. I'm not for one second saying my parents didn't love me. They were probably just too busy to want to help. Maybe my problems weren't as important as theirs.

I am also not going to absolve myself from all responsibility. I admit it: I was the class clown. My mistake was that I thought it was a good thing to make other people laugh. It didn't matter where and it didn't matter when. I just liked to be funny. It was only in my later teens that I had to accept that there was a time and place for everything.

The classroom was not the place to try and be funny. My football coach, who was also my sixth-class teacher, went out of his way to embarrass me in front of everyone. Whether he would attack me for looking like my hair wasn't done or mock my inability to read out aloud fluently, that's how he got his kicks. Dennis Coglan was his name. What an arsehole. Like everyone who made fun of me, all I wanted to do was make them like me but I didn't know how. Many years later, Dennis moved into the house behind us. He never changed. When Mum or Dad were around he was polite and kind. When I was on my own, he'd ridicule me over something I did or said. As I said, what an arsehole.

In high school, I was in the hockey side – no questions. I again tried out for football. I made the rugby side but the league side was full of the usual suspects from primary school, and they hadn't changed.

* * * *

The thing is, I was, and still am, very average. I was reasonably popular with the girls but not enough for any of them to want to go out with me. Maybe it was because I was a quirky-looking guy. I was certainly no oil painting and my personality did have flaws, although I don't know if that's because I was trying too hard to be liked. Everyone tells me beauty is only skin deep so it couldn't have been the quirky thing. I think it was the confidence, or lack of it. I was shy and reserved – two very unattractive qualities to a woman.

I was actually chased by two different girls in Year 11 but, if you're not attracted, you're not attracted. It does go both ways. Maybe I thought I deserved better. It doesn't matter what I thought, I was obviously incapable of achieving my ambitions when it came to girls.

There was a party one weekend and I was told by one of my mates that I had to go because Lorraine was going to be there and wanted to 'get it on' with me. That scared me shitless. I was that insecure within myself that I didn't go because, if she wanted to have sex with me, I was afraid of doing something stupid and embarrassing myself. That's how bad it got. I wanted to have sex so bad because everyone else talked about how good it was but, at the end of the day, I was 'chicken'. No, it had nothing to do with the values I had been brought up with. I wanted to get laid – I just wasn't ready.

I had always thought I was a bit of a magnet: unfortunately, not with the chicks, but with the bullies. Throughout high school it seemed to be amplified. Anyone who went to Chatham High School from 1978 to 1981 would remember the guy who used to bring his hockey stick to school even though it was cricket season. That was me. It got to a point where I thought I had actually brought the bullying upon myself. By carrying a hockey stick, I was taunting them to have a go at me. It was too much for them not to have a go. Between the hockey stick and the steel capped boots, I used to keep them at bay.

I can honestly say that I never intentionally did anything to make me a target, but I was. Some kids are just like that. I was one of them. Comparatively, I was a big guy. I was six foot tall at fifteen years old; however, I wasn't strong, so I couldn't defend myself, especially when there were three or four on one.

My mum worked at the school. I know it's bad for a mum to intervene in a son's problems, but there were so many things she could have done to stop the rot. She did nothing. The teachers were almost as bad as the other kids … she did nothing. That always saddened me.

I was falsely accused by a teacher of misbehaving on a school excursion and therefore excluded from representing the school in a rugby game. Mum didn't stand up for me. I had to do that myself. Maybe that was her plan. It didn't work. I had been standing up for myself my whole life, only to be kicked and beaten back to the ground. I had played the whole competition for the school and, because they thought I did something wrong, they cut me from the grand final, which was a draw. To make matters worse, I was not acknowledged as a contributor to the team and they left me out of the team photo. Forevermore, I have no proof that I was a member of that team. I was always very proud to represent my school; this was a real kick in the teeth. Only in my heart I know the truth.

I think that that period in my life was the first time I had ever thought of killing myself. I think that young people committing suicide over the atrocious acts of cyber bullying today is bad enough, but I look back at what I had to go through and I honestly can't believe that I didn't kill myself. I used to think of how I'd do it. I even used to think I was a coward for not going through with it. At one stage,

I took a sharp carving knife from the kitchen draw and placed it just below my sternum and pressed. I knew that once it initially pierced the skin, it would just sink deep into me. Obviously, I couldn't do it.

* * * *

I left school after Year 10. It was 1981. I couldn't get out of that place quick enough. It's ironic because, looking back, I enjoyed being at school with my mates, but that was it. I wasn't a scholar but I enjoyed recess, lunch, and sport. I'm not saying for a minute that I'm unintelligent. I just lacked the will to apply myself. I would rather have fun than study.

I thought I wanted to become a builder. I enjoyed working with timber. Even as a youngster, I had spent time with my cousin Keith at his workshop and he'd give me tasks to do. I thought I had the aptitude so I attended a pre-apprenticeship course in Wauchope.

Although my work was exceptional and my assignments were very good, my desire to be a builder took a nosedive. For some reason, there were certain tasks that I couldn't grasp. I kept at them but I just couldn't absorb the concepts. The TAFE teacher lost patience with me. I would have as well. He started to treat me harshly. I could see this negative pattern emerging again until, one day I referred to him as 'Dick Head', which was very close to his name. I knew it was the wrong thing to say as soon as I said it, but I was frustrated as well. Not with him but with myself. In front of everyone, he grabbed me by the scruff of the neck and pushed me down a ramp on a building site. I grabbed my hammer and threw it at him, causing him to lose balance and fall over. That was the end of that.

Growing Up

I left TAFE and decided that I'd take the rest of the year off and think about what I wanted to do. In the meantime, I worked for my dad at the sawmill he managed. I'm sure he gave me every shit job under the sun just to ram home to me what life would be like for me if I didn't get my act together. I decided then that, given my lot in life was to be bullied, I'd join the police force so that I could help people who couldn't help themselves.

In the meantime, Scrubby Towers and I went on a trip to Bali on a surfing holiday. Scrubby was a friend of mine. We first met because of our love for trail bike riding and surfing. Scrubby was his nickname because, well frankly, he looked a bit 'scrubby' all the time, but he was a great bloke. It was the first holiday abroad for both of us. We had two weeks over there. It was amazing!

A funny thing happened on our first day. We were staying in a little shack in Legion Beach. Not knowing much about Bali, we got up, stuck our wetsuits on, and rushed to the beach. The sand was boiling hot; the water wasn't much better. We looked at each other as everyone else was looking at us. Damn, it was hot! We raced back to the shack, ripped our wetsuits off, and went back down to the beach. Much better! Another Aussie bloke, Tyrone, said, 'First time to Bali, hey?' and he laughed. After two weeks, I thought that it was a great experience but I really wanted to go home. I love Australia. It truly is the best country on earth.

* * * *

In 1983, I went back to school to do Years 11 and 12 at Chatham High School. My original class was now in Year 12. Although we often crossed paths, we almost never spoke. It was if I had never existed. I became much closer to my new Year 11 class. Although I still hadn't shaken the 'class clown' mentality, I was a little more reserved. I still liked to be funny but I toned it down. I found that my new class – who didn't really know the old me – had sort of accepted me as one of their own. The girls took a while – about twelve months; however, in Year 12, I got to know and love them. I honestly don't know what they thought of me though. They were the best group of people I had known up until that point in my life. My only sadness was that I only got to spend two years of my school life with them.

Later, the thought occurred to me that perhaps the bullying I used to suffer happened purely because I was younger than the bullies and they saw me as weak. Or did it simply occur because I was seen as a smartarse? I didn't know then and I don't know now. I do suspect though, that it was the latter. I don't suffer fools lightly and have never been backward in voicing an opinion, no matter how abruptly it may come across. I also love admitting when I'm wrong because, frankly, it's a novelty. You see, I don't talk out of my backside. I voice opinions based on all of the relevant information I have on the topic at the time; what I read, what I hear, what I see, and what I remember.

I have always done things that have gotten me into trouble, like the 'Chris Cusford incident' where I left him behind in the water. I didn't think it through properly then; however, I still knew it was wrong. There are other things that I've done that can't be included in this book purely for legal reasons. Have I made bad choices? Definitely! Am I a bad person because of those choices? I don't think so but that's not for me to judge.

In 1983, I was playing 'B' grade hockey for the Group 3 Leagues Club. My brother was the goalie for the 'A' grade side and my mate, Leonard, was the goalie for the 'C' grade side. It was a great year for the club and for me personally. All three grades had won the minor premiership. My brother was off to university the following year and I was being considered to succeed him as the 'A' grade goalie.

Grand final day came around and there was a buzz in the air about the possibility of the club being the first in the history of the Manning Valley to win both the minor and major premierships in the same year in all three grades. 'C' grade was first up and everyone gathered to watch them score a convincing win over their opposition – Tigers. It was a three – nil score line that set the scene for the other two grades.

My team was next up. I've gotta say, I was calm. I knew we had the wood over Tigers and, in my mind, it was only the score line that was in question. As it turned out, Tigers turned up to play that day. It was by far the busiest I had been in the goals in a long time. They were peppering shots at me like there was no tomorrow. Late in the first half, a penalty stroke was awarded against our fullback. I can't remember what for but, nonetheless, I was a bit nervous. Yet, at the same time, I had a very good record for defending penalty strokes and so I felt quietly confident.

As the Tigers forward approached the spot, I took my position on the line. It's one of those times you feel the whole world watching you: probably because they are. I took a moment, then placed myself on the line, slightly left of centre. I always did this so that the striker would see the wider gap to shoot for. It also gave me a better than average chance at picking the direction he would choose.

I set myself, looking him in the eye. He moved in, stepped into the ball, and scooped it to my right. The ball was lightning fast. I dived to my right but, in the process, dislodged my hockey stick from my right hand, fouling it on my pads. I stopped the ball by deflecting it wide with my right hand. It hit the post and bounced away. I managed to grab my stick with my left hand before it hit the ground. I had saved our team once again. A cheer went up from the crowd and I looked to my dad and brother who were standing behind me. They both gave me a nod of approval.

The second half was as intense as the first with the goalies from both sides having to make save after save to keep our respective sides in the game. With fifteen minutes to go, I cleared a ball straight up the centre of the field. A Tigers defender miss-trapped the ball which resulted in a long corner. The corner was taken quickly and passed to Glen Watson in the centre of the field. Brilliantly, he worked his way into the goal circle where he struck the ball hard, firing it into the back of the goal. I remember hearing the 'clunk, clunk' as the ball hit the side board and then the backboard of the goal. The scream went up from the whole team and sticks flew into the air with glee. I couldn't contain my excitement. The Tigers team dropped their heads. They couldn't believe it. The crowd continued to cheer until we were all back on side ready for the re-start. The opposition wasn't happy but they weren't giving up either.

It was the longest fifteen minutes of my life – I didn't just stand there twiddling my thumbs. Tigers were determined to level the score. They continued coming at us with everything they had. Shot after shot they fired at me and time after time I deflected, scooped away, blocked, dived, and cleared everything they threw at me. In the last two minutes, we had two penalty corners awarded against us. On the second, they had just had their shot and I cleared the ball when I heard two loud blasts of the umpire's whistle. I looked at the umpire and he was pointing to the centre of the ground. It was over.

It was surreal. I ran to my teammates and we knew that that was the best game of hockey we had ever played and we had come out on the other side victorious. It is true that we were expected to win but we were expected to win easily. Somebody had forgotten to tell Tigers. Any other day and they may have won, but on that day we were playing to make history and we kept our end of the bargain. That day was our day. It was now up to my brother's 'A' grade side to make the legend come true.

As it turned out, they did. They beat Taree West three – one in a thrilling end to a thrilling day. I couldn't help but give my brother a bit of stick – pardon the pun – for being the only goalie to let in a goal. Just couldn't help myself. After the game, we went back to the leagues club and then on to Johnny Taylor's house for the after party. It was one of the best days of my life.

There was a write-up in the local paper about our club's achievement and, in particular, I received a short mention about my performance on the day. 'In B-Grade, Mitchell Walton, not to be outdone by his A-Grade counterpart and brother, Max, had an outstanding game. He saved many Tigers' shots at goal and the team can thank him for the premiership.'

Proud doesn't begin to describe how I felt. To this day, I consider that my crowning glory. Not a 'biggy' in the grand scheme of things but it taught me one thing that, up until then, I hadn't realised. If you work hard in whatever you do the rewards will come, but you will have to work at it. Nobody is going to hand you success on a platter.

The next year, I was promoted to 'A' grade. The pace was so much faster and so much more intense than 'B' grade. Later in the season, we were nearing the finals and we weren't playing well. On one particular day, one of the umpires was from the same club as the opposition we were facing. I was getting very frustrated with the poor quality of his umpiring.

Late in the game, we were one – nil down. The opposition shot a ball into the circle. It was waist-high and should have been called up as dangerous, but the dodgy umpire let it go. It hit me in the upper thigh and dropped into my pad. The umpire called a penalty corner. I got the shits and threw my stick at him. He called me over and issued a yellow card, placing me in the sin bin for five minutes. As I walked past him, I 'lightly' punched him in the mouth. He then changed his decision to a red card. Again, I knew I had done the wrong thing immediately. I also knew that I was in the shit. It doesn't matter what sport you play … never touch an umpire.

I had to front the judiciary and, despite an unblemished record, they suspended me from the game for five years. I later learned that the maximum they could impose was only two years so I appealed and had it reduced. Still, I was ashamed of my actions on that day. I let my parents down, I let my team mates down but, most of all, I let myself down.

Anyway, I had my Higher School Certificate to concentrate on. I gave myself plenty of time to study but also plenty of time to play. During those two years of Years 11 and 12 I felt so easy within myself. It was how school life is supposed to be; not a bully, no trouble, not a care. On our last official day of school before the exams started, we played a grudge match of rugby league between Years 11 and 12. During the game, I was heavily tackled from the side, snapping my lateral ligaments clean off the bone in my right knee. I didn't know it was broken at the time but it hurt like a bitch. It put a real dent in my exam preparations. The knee specialist informed me that my knee required surgery, but he couldn't do anything until the swelling went down and the infection was under control. That meant waiting in hospital.

On the Saturday night, the band 'Mental as Anything' was playing at the RSL club. Everyone was going to be there except me. I'd already bought my ticket weeks before so I thought it was wasted. Early in the evening of the night of the performance, Leonard turned up at the hospital. I explained to the nurse that I needed to go to the concert but she steadfastly refused to grant my request. I accepted that I'd miss it but Leonard had other ideas. He rounded up a wheelchair and we snuck out of the ward, down the elevator, out to the street, down the road, and to the RSL. I thought, *Great, here I am. Now what?*

Leonard had organised with the security staff for me to watch the band from the balcony. It was actually the poolroom overlooking the auditorium. It was great. All my friends came up to see me. It was like I was a VIP. At the end of the night, we had all had a bit too much to drink.

Then came the hard part – getting back to the hospital ward without being seen.

Leonard was pushing me in my wheelchair down the middle of the street. Faster and faster we went. I could feel the wind rushing through my hair. I didn't know if I was having fun or shitting myself. Sometimes, when we went out together, the two were one and the same.

It didn't occur to me at the time that the nurses knew I wasn't there about half an hour after we had snuck out. Anyway, after they tore me a new one, they were quite nice to me again. I actually had a snog with one of the nurses some months later at another band. Ahhh, Michelle!

I did my first English exam in hospital the day after my knee operation. I had an epidural so that I wouldn't be groggy for the exam. That was an experience; being awake as they hammered away at my knee. The things the doctors and nurses talked about were so matter-of-fact; like they were talking to a friend at the pub as though I wasn't even there. I do remember thinking to myself, *This is going to hurt like a bitch when the anesthetic wears off.* I wasn't wrong. I was doped up on so much pain medication that I spewed all over my English paper. It was probably gibberish anyway.

I got out of hospital and continued to study. After all, I couldn't do anything else for a couple of weeks. At the end of exams when everybody went their own way, it was very sad for me. While it was an exciting time for everyone, I was very confused about what was going to happen to me from that point.

I had to get a score of 221 out of 500 to get into the police force. Those were the days when you didn't need to be an academic to be a police officer. You just needed common sense – something today's police lack. When the results came out I was stunned. I opened the envelope and looked at the score. I couldn't believe it ... 221. I was elated but I also thought it was too close to risk. I immediately lodged an appeal on the grounds of misadventure, given the knee thing.

Several weeks later, I received a letter from the board of studies giving me an extra ten points – 231. That was enough to do what I'd gone back to school to do. I believe I could have done a lot better considering my trial yielded me a score of 319, and I didn't study for that either.

* * * *

It was at that stage that I decided to move to Sydney. I knew there was work down there so off I went. For the first time in my life, I was in control of me. Nobody else was pulling the strings anymore.

In 1985, I was twenty and still hadn't had a girlfriend. After moving to Sydney in the inner west, that was high on my list. Get a flat – tick. Get a job – tick. Get a girlfriend – working on it. I still had this shyness thing to get over.

I didn't have much money and so I moved into a small ground-floor flat in the inner-west suburb of Croydon Park with my mate Leonard. Leonard was a fairly short man with red hair and a cheesy smile. We had been through school together, played hockey together, water-skied together, snow-skied together, gone clubbing together, and got up to mischief together. Leonard was the exact opposite to me in the extreme. His personality was on fire. A more confident man you will never encounter.

Leonard and I had a great life. We were both twenty and looking to live life to the fullest. 'No regrets' was our motto. He had a promising career as a manager with Kmart Tyre and Auto. I applied to the police force. Due to the injury I sustained on the final day of school the previous year, I had to ensure I was in peek physical condition before the police force would accept me. So I spent many hours training, playing sport, and getting fit. After doing the physical exam and passing with ease, I only had the aptitude test and the referee interviews to go. I was nearly there but, in the meantime, there was one other thing that I lacked – money.

In the first few weeks after moving to Sydney, I applied for many jobs and received many job offers in return. It was a great period in Australia as there were often more jobs available than there were people to fill them. At least that's how I recall it, as I never had a problem getting work. Since I had my heart set on becoming a policeman, I didn't want to take any job that would make me think twice about leaving to achieve my goal. I even knocked back a job as flight attendant with Qantas. Idiot!

My very first job was with my cousin, Keith. He owned K & R Kitchens at Chipping Norton. K & R stood for Keith and Rheina. Rheina was a doctor and was lovely. Keith taught me how to laminate bench tops and assemble kitchen cabinets. I couldn't afford a car at the time, so it was up at 4.00 am every morning to catch the train from Ashfield in Sydney's inner west. Keith would pick me up from Cabramatta Train Station for the final leg into work at Chipping Norton. I didn't mind because I was working for someone I idolised.

Keith was larger than life. He made me feel that I had worth. He made me feel that I could achieve anything. He even taught me how to water-ski. The man was my hero.

When I was around twelve, Keith used to take me to their little shack on the Hawkesbury River at Sackville at Christmas time to spend a week having the time of my life. I must admit, I had a bit of a crush on Rheina so it wasn't that hard to accept his invitation. It was ok to have a crush on your cousin's wife at that age.

Shortly after starting work with Keith, he bought a brand new Brock Commodore. This disgusted me. I was a Ford man and so were half of the crew that worked for him. One of the guys had a hotted-up XC Falcon. It was a stunning car. One day, Keith and Stuart had a bet with each other as to whose car was the fastest. I thought Keith's car would shit all over Stuart's Falcon but I couldn't bet against the Ford. I didn't have it in me. One afternoon, we all knocked off early to go down a back street in Chipping Norton so the two could have it out.

Never let your heart rule your head when it comes to money. Keith's Commodore blitzed it. He won by half a car length. I thought because I was young, stupid, and his cousin, he'd let me off the hook. Yeah right! Cough it up, Mitchy-boy. Twenty-five dollars. On my wage back then, that was heaps.

* * * *

Keith and Rheina had a very good group of friends who were always playing practical jokes. We were over at the Sackville Gardens Caravan Park sneaking a shower one night. One of their friends –Chris – was in the shower. I dumped a bucket of icy-cold water over the top of the cubicle on him. He nearly shit himself. Keith and I couldn't stop laughing. Keith had this laugh that was amazing. He hardly made a sound but he looked like he was about to explode with rapturous joy. Keith thought it was very funny, but I knew I had better be prepared because Chris wouldn't be letting it go at that. My mistake was that I did it too early in the week. I then spent the rest of the week looking over my shoulder and sleeping with one eye open.

Every time I looked at Chris, he had this dirty great grin on his face. On the last day, we were cleaning up and getting ready to go home when he asked me to go and get a bucket of water from the river to flush the toilets out before we left. I went and got a bucket of water and handed it to him. He turned and walked back up to the shack, so I went and had a seat next to Keith on the water's edge.

We were chatting away when, suddenly, I felt like I was at the bottom of a waterfall. In front of me sat a twenty-litre empty bucket – the one I had gone to get the water in for Chris. Keith had known it was coming because he made a sudden dash at the last minute. I looked up and there was Chris, sporting a grin that reached from ear to ear. Revenge is a dish best served cold they say! The worst part was that I did all the hard work to get the bucket of water for him. We were even ... until next time. Little did I know at that stage, there would be no next time.

I was working for Keith for about three months when I received a job offer with a company at Lakemba – George Hudson Parquetry Floors. I didn't even know what parquetry was when I applied for the job. I just knew that I loved working with wood. I told Keith I was leaving and he did what any idol would do. He gave me a big hug, shook my hand, thanked me for helping him, and wished me luck.

* * * *

I really enjoyed getting up and going to work each day. I was learning a trade that would serve me well off and on for the next twenty years. I would go to work and come home absolutely knackered, but I was happy. I had money at last, and I could pay rent and buy the things that I wanted without sponging off my parents.

Leonard and I would plan what we were going to do on the weekends and our lives were never dull. We played indoor hockey at Bankstown. We played outdoor hockey for Ryde – Hunters Hill on Saturdays, although, I had to play under an assumed name – Mitch Matthews – because my two-year suspension was still in place. It was ok but, really, I had lost the passion I once had for the game, so I only played for a season.

Leonard was very good with the ladies. I don't know why they liked him; he was an annoying person at times but, hey, so was I. He never had a problem getting a date when he didn't want to hang out with me. I, on the other hand, always felt nervous around girls. I had never had a girlfriend and, at that stage had never had sex; not with anyone else anyway. I'd been out on dates before and had encounters, but never had the confidence to step up, hit the ball, and slide into home base. I didn't realise at the time, but I think the girls I used to date wanted a 'bad boy' type of guy, and I certainly wasn't that. I had been taught by my parents to treat girls with respect and to treat them like ladies; the old fashioned way. Unfortunately for me, the old fashioned way wasn't the way to get lucky. Maybe it was just my lack of confidence? I'll never know.

One night, Leonard, his little brother, Clint, and I went out for a drive in my old beat-up Subaru Leone. It was red. Nothing worked except the engine and every panel was dented. It had cost me a hundred bucks. Clint wanted to stop and call his girlfriend, Rose. I kept telling him to shut up and pull his head in. He could call her later. Anyway, the nagging just got too much for me so I pulled up to a phone box in Leichardt. Clint got out and was in the phone box for about ten minutes. We were calling him to hurry up. I got the shits. I told Leonard to hang on, started the car, put it in reverse, and tromped it.

I reversed into the phone box with Clint still in it. I knocked it off its mounts and it fell on its side and collapsed like a cardboard box with the ends removed. Dangerous? Yes. Hilarious? Definitely. It was the funniest thing you have ever seen because Clint, laying inside this collapsed phone box, kept talking to Rose as if nothing had happened. That was the nature of the relationship between Leonard, Clint, and me. We looked up and saw an old man sitting on his front veranda in a rocking chair, slowly shaking his head. We had to go. I could hear sirens.

CHAPTER TWO

I was sitting at home alone one night watching television when I looked out of the lounge room window to the top unit of the block behind us. There was an attractive girl doing the dishes. She looked at me and waved. I waved back. She was very pleasing on the eye and I kept looking up at her. I couldn't help it. To my amazement, she kept smiling and looking back. Her hair was pure blonde, medium length, straight, and immaculately brushed. I loved that look. She looked at me once more, gave me a smile, and then left the window. I thought, *Oh well, she's going to bed or going to watch TV.* Instead, she came out onto her balcony and beckoned me to open my window.

I opened my window and looked up at her.

She said, 'How are you?'

I said, 'Good thanks.'

She asked in a cheery voice, 'What's your name?'

'Mitchell, what's yours?'

'Missy,' she replied.

I remember thinking immediately, *She looks like a 'Missy'*. Her voice was mid-range in pitch and distinctly feminine. Coupled with the fact that she was very easy on the eye. I thought she was hot.

I said, 'What are you doing?'

'Just finished the dishes and my flat-mate's out, so I might go to bed.'

'Same,' I said.

'I've been waving at you for a while. I was wondering how long it would take you to notice.'

With a little chuckle, I said, 'I don't usually stalk my neighbours through the window.' She laughed.

We chatted about this and that for a short while until she finally said goodnight and went inside. My immediate thought was that I liked her, but that she must have gotten bored with the conversation and given herself an 'out' by going inside – my insecurity raising its ugly head again.

The next night, same thing. But, this time, Leonard was home as well. She was doing the dishes and when she had finished she came out onto the balcony and beckoned for me to talk to her. Again, I opened the window and we started to chat. Leonard opened the other window and invited her down to our unit. I thought to myself, *Thanks, Leonard. I would never have had the courage to do that.*

A few moments later, there was a knock at the door. I opened it and this beautiful girl, about eighteen or nineteen, stood in the doorway with a smile that seemed to light up the small, dimly-lit foyer. At the time, I thought it would have lit up the Sydney Entertainment Centre. I invited her in and we all sat down to find out a bit more about each other.

During the conversation, I could feel the mood change between Leonard and me. I knew he was trying to impress Missy with his stories and experiences and I felt that I was being left on the outer. What I did notice though, was that she was constantly looking back at me. I knew then that she liked me but didn't know how to reciprocate with

Leonard there. Leonard was dominating the conversation and I could tell she was being polite by giving him the attention he wanted. After about an hour, I realised that I wouldn't be able to get a word in edgeways, so I asked Missy if she would like a drink. She declined. Instead, she stood and said that she had to go. Leonard offered to walk her to her unit, which she refused at first, then accepted, as Leonard wouldn't take no for an answer.

On his return, he told me that he thought that she liked him and that 'he was in'. Typical Leonard –jumping the gun again. I knew he wasn't serious about Missy because he had a longtime girlfriend in Armidale ... Rachelle.

Rachelle was studying to be a teacher. I had always liked Rachelle and, one night at the Taree RSL when she and Leonard were on a 'break', I nearly broke the 'Bro Code'. You know. Never go where a mate has been. It's just not the done thing. We had both had a little too much to drink and had gotten to a point of comfort with each other. We were standing quite close, talking and looking into each other's eyes in a 'non-friend' kind of way I thought. It could easily have happened. The only thing that ruined it for me – or saved me (depending on how you look at it) – was my inconsiderate sister, Sasha. She was spewing her guts up in the trough in the men's toilets. There's nothing worse than having long blonde hair that smells like a urinal. Needless to say, Rachelle went without that night, and not to be too presumptuous, so did I.

It would have been really weird having Rachelle as my first. We were mates, which goes completely against my theory. Under the right circumstances, a straight man will always try to crack onto a woman. But there are definitely wrong circumstances. For example, I like my mate's wife as a friend but I would never go there; however, if she wasn't married to my mate and I wasn't married, it's game on. Obviously there has to be an attraction, but it's amazing how much alcohol makes both sides more attractive to each another.

The day after Missy's visit to our flat, nothing happened; no dishes being washed, no balcony chat. I was disappointed. I went to work on Saturday to do some overtime and worked my butt off. It was a great day though. I was feeling good and, when I knocked off, I wanted to go home, have a shower, get dressed, and go into the city for a night out. Instead, it was the night that changed my life forever.

When I got home, I decided to sit for five minutes while I worked out where we were going to go. Leonard arrived home and said he had a shit day and wanted to stay in. I had nobody else to go out with so we agreed to stay in.

Around six o'clock, I heard Missy.

'Mitch, are you there?' It was funny really but cheaper than a phone call.

I looked up and saw Missy standing on her balcony. It was a real Romeo and Juliette moment. I opened up the window. 'Hello,' I said.

'I need a really big favour,' she replied, sounding needy.

She wanted me to drive her into the city to pick up her friend from a hotel in Ultimo. She explained that she had injured her foot and couldn't drive. Leonard was in his room, so I told him I was taking Missy into the city to pick up her friend. Big mistake; he invited himself along. Just when I thought I could have some alone time with Missy. Idiot!

The 'One'

My car wasn't the best so we took Leonard's Gemini. He ushered Missy into the front passenger seat, which consequently put me in the back. Great. Anyway, we got to the hotel in Ultimo where Missy's friend was. Missy started to get out of the car.

I said, 'Don't, Missy, I'll go. What's her name?'

'Jann.'

I got out of the car and walked into the front bar of the hotel. There weren't many people in there but there was a solo guitarist playing 'American Pie'. I love that song. I was watching him play, noting how good he was, when I noticed this girl lying face down on a bar stool ... swimming. She had a great stroke technique. My dad used to coach swimmers so I had been around a pool a lot when I was younger. She was 'very happy' and seemed to be having a good time with her friends. To carry over the pub noise, I asked in a rather loud voice, 'IS THERE A JANN IN THE ROOM?'

The Olympic swimmer looked up at me, lost her balance, and fell off the chair. She looked up at me again and said, 'Yep, that's me.'

I said, 'C'mon, let's go.'

She said in an inquisitive, yet mischievous, voice, 'Who the hell are YOU?'

'I'm Missy's friend. She's outside in the car.'

'Ahhh. Missy's told me about you,' she said, in a slow smiley voice.

I helped Jann up and escorted her to the car and into the back seat. She was quite drunk but very happy. She couldn't sit up straight and asked if she could lay her head on my lap. I said, 'No worries.'

She put her head in my lap for a while and then she looked up at me. Our eyes met and she gave me a slight smile, like the one you get from someone who is attracted to you and wants your attention. I returned the compliment. I knew immediately ... this would be the girl I would fall in love with. I don't know how that happened so quickly. There was just a 'thing' about her that captured me at that moment. I gently stroked her hair back out of her eyes and she closed her eyes and took my other hand and held it in hers.

We got home and I helped Missy take Jann up the stairs to their unit. As we were standing at the door, I said, 'Would you like me to help you take her inside?'

Missy said quickly, 'No, I don't think so. I'll be fine.' I think at that stage, Missy sensed my interest in Jann.

The next day, I had to work in the morning. Although I never usually work on a Sunday, I needed the money. I was quite annoyed at having to work but I was home by midday. As soon as I got home, I looked up at the girl's balcony. They were both there. My mood changed immediately. I opened the window. Missy said 'Hi', and Jann said 'Hi', in a sheepish or embarrassed sort of tone.

I said, 'How are you feeling today?'

Missy said, 'I'm fine thanks.'

I said, 'I meant Jann.'

Jann said, 'I'm ok. A little embarrassed though. Sorry about that.'

I said, 'Don't be. You were good entertainment. Do you both want to come down?' I asked them both down because I knew that Leonard would occupy Missy while I could get to know the girl behind those beautiful eyes.

'Sure,' came the reply from Jann.

A few moments later, there was a knock on the door. I opened the door and there stood Missy, looking very nice as usual, and Jann, in a pair of trackie daks, t-shirt, and no shoes. I was gone. I thought she looked so gorgeous and cute. I invited them in and we sat and talked for about an hour, finding out things like where she was from, where she went to school, and what she was studying at university.

Jann was a country girl who came from a large property near Collarenebri in the north-west of New South Wales. She was the daughter of a farming family, which included her brother. Her parents, Judy and David, farmed sheep and wheat. She was sent to a private boarding school at the age of fourteen and came home between school terms, but she missed that bonding between her and her parents that most of us take for granted. She also attended pony club. This is a big deal in the outback as it provides a valuable social outlet for young people who would otherwise, due to distance, miss out on the social interaction so readily available to their city counterparts.

Jann and Missy were both studying nursing. They were inseparable. Jann and I had common taste in music and so I thought that may be my opportunity. Over the next week, we were chatting more and more through the window. I knew that Jimmy Barnes was playing at the State Sports Centre at Homebush. I asked Jann if she'd like to go and she said she'd love to. I had never felt so good in my life. I thought, *I have found a girl who likes me. She lives next door. She's beautiful, smart, and funny, and she makes me feel so good when we're together.*

It was an agonising wait for our first date but I was really looking forward to it.

* * * *

In the meantime, a good mate from Taree came and stayed with us. Thomas was his name. He was a mechanic and a wizard with all things mechanical. In fact, a wizard with anything, except knowing when he was being gee'd up. Leonard, Clint, Thomas, and I went out in Sydney one night for a bit of fun. We were in Chinatown having dinner in an upstairs restaurant when I had an idea.

I told the guys I was going to the toilet. I got up and went down the stairs a bit. I caught Clint's eye and beckoned him to come with me. He got up and came over. I told him what I was doing so he went back over to the table and whispered the plan to Leonard. Leonard got up and told Thomas he was going to the toilet and then came over to me. Clint told Thomas he was going to call his girlfriend and all three of us left the restaurant leaving Thomas behind, knowing he couldn't afford the bill. Every now and again, we'd sneak back up the stairs to see what was going on. He looked decidedly nervous when the restaurant staff bailed him up as he was trying to leave. It was so funny watching him try to get out of a sticky situation like that. I could see him looking around for a way to escape. I didn't want him jumping over the balcony so we ended up going back and paying the bill. He'd nearly shit himself.

* * * *

It wasn't long before our date night was upon us. A big group of us had organised to go together to ease the 'first date' tension. I was as nervous as hell. We were all having a great time. Jimmy was as powerful as ever, thumping out the tunes. The atmosphere was tremendous. Then he started to sing one of my favourite songs, 'Working Class Man'. As it happened, it was one of Jann's favourites as well.

All the guys were putting their girlfriends on their shoulders and I decided to do the same. We were dancing around when I suddenly felt faint. Jann was clenching her thighs around my neck so tight to stop from falling that she cut off the circulation to my head. I fainted, toppling like a falling tree. Way to go, Mitch! The next thing I remembered was waking up behind the stage in the ambulance room with Jann looking down on me. She had a big smile on her face. I said, 'Now we're even.' She laughed, took me by the hand and, after getting the all-clear from the ambos, we went back out to watch the remainder of the show.

On the way home, Jann and I were in the back seat of the car and she started to fall asleep. *There is a pattern emerging here*, I thought. I put my arm around her and pulled her close. She looked at me, smiled, and snuggled up. I was in love. When we arrived back at my place, we got out of the car and I started to walk her back to her unit. We only took three steps when I turned and kissed her. It was so sensual. I felt warm all over. My body was tingling with excitement. My heart was pounding out through my chest. All I could think about was that she must be into me as much as I was into her.

We kissed for what seemed like an eternity, then I put my arm around her and walked her to her unit. We kissed again at her front door and she said, 'I had a great night. Thank you.'

I said, 'Me too. You are so beautiful.'

She gave me a hug and said, 'I'll talk to you tomorrow.' She then went inside, turned and smiled at me and, after a short pause, closed the door.

As I walked back to my unit I knew: this was the girl of my dreams. She was the girl I wanted to spend the rest of my life loving. I didn't know yet how profound that thought would later turn out to be.

My relationship with Jann began to develop and I was feeling pretty good about myself. One night, Leonard was upstairs smoking cones with a guy from State Rail. Cool guy; very laid back for a white guy. There was a knock on the door. When I opened it, it was Jann, standing there in her pyjamas. I took her by the hand and we sat on the lounge.

We had only talked for a little while but I couldn't control myself any longer. I leant over and kissed her. She pulled away and looked into my eyes before kissing me again. It was very passionate and tender. Her lips were so soft. Her eyes sparkled like crystals in the moonlight. We lay down on the couch, kissing, caressing, stroking each other, until she took my hand and placed it under her shirt and on her breasts. This was the first time I had ever touched a woman like this and I tell you it felt great. I was gentle; softly touching her. I could feel myself becoming more aroused. I knew she could feel my hardness pressing against her. She had her hand on my chest, then she started to slide it slowly down my body towards my rock-hard member.

Our lips parted and she said in a soft, vulnerable voice, 'Am I just going to be another notch in your bedpost?'

I looked into her eyes and said, 'You'd be the first notch in my bedpost.'

'Fair dink?' she asked in a surprised tone.

'Fair dink,' I replied.

Jann sat up. I thought that she was about to leave, traumatised by the responsibility of taking a man's virginity. However, instead, she stood, took my hand, led me to my bedroom, turned back the bed covers, and lay down on the bed, gently pulling me towards her.

I kissed her again and started to unbutton her pyjama top. I pulled it apart to expose her beautifully-shaped breasts. I then slid my fingers under the waistband of her pyjama bottoms and slowly drew them down until she was lying there completely naked. I'd seen pictures in magazines before but I could not believe how beautiful a female body could be. Jann was like a goddess to me, lying there waiting for me to undress and join her. I sat down beside her and she removed my shirt. She put her hand inside my pants and touched me there. I removed my pants and lay down beside her.

I kissed her again. The warmth of her body against mine was sublime. She took my hand and slid it slowly down her body towards her devil's playground. I thought to myself, *What a contradiction. For a devil's playground, it is very, very heavenly.* The soft curls of her pubic hair, the warmth of her inner thighs, and the wetness of her pussy were alluring. I was rubbing her so gently and I could hear her start to moan. As her body started to move around, her excitement built. She took my hand and pushed my fingers inside her while at the same time gently curling her hand around my penis, sliding it up and down.

She looked at me and said, 'I want you inside me ... Now!' I got on top of her and she guided me into her. As I entered her, she moaned even louder and, at the same time, she wrapped her legs around me, pulling me deeper into her.

Just when I thought life couldn't get any better than this, I felt what could only be described as an imminent building of excitement and passion within me. I couldn't help it. I began to thrust harder and faster ... deeper. She was gazing into my eyes the whole time, making this the most erotic moment in history. Suddenly, she came. Her body was shivering; like she was cold; but she was definitely not cold. I couldn't hold it in any longer. My body felt like a saucepan of boiling water with the lid on. My body actually felt like it was boiling. The pressure was intense until I erupted. I could feel myself pulsating inside of her. I couldn't believe what had just happened to me.

The feeling of ecstasy slowly subsided. My arms turned to jelly trying to hold myself up, so I lowered myself down on top of her, still inside her. I kissed her again and again, lightly but passionately. We rolled to the side, never breaking our gaze into each other's eyes. There were no words. We just lay there until she said, 'How are you?'

'That was amazing! Why wasn't I told about this sooner? How long's this been going on?' I said, still panting. I didn't even have the energy to laugh.

I didn't mean for her to leave, but I told her Leonard would be home soon and I didn't want him to see us. I'd forgotten to lock the door. No sooner had the words left my mouth and Jann was up and back in her pyjamas. I got dressed as well and walked her home. It was a silent walk. Many things were rushing though my head. We got to her door and she asked me if I wanted to stay over. I was surprised but happy. I stayed the night and we made love twice more before morning.

The 'One'

On waking in the morning, I lay there watching her as she slept. I had never seen anybody so beautiful. My emotions were running rampant. Then I had a funny thought. I'd broken so many personal records that night ... first time I had sex, first time I had a sleepover, first time I had sex three times in one night. I was on fire. I watched her until her eyes opened. She smiled and kissed me. We lay there and cuddled for a while, still naked.

She asked, 'How was that?'

I replied, 'That was fantastic, Jann. I can't believe how good that was.'

'You want to go again or do you want brekky?'

I nodded. This time, it was just raw passionate sex.

She said, 'You're a big boy, Mitch.'

I knew that I was just average, but she knew just what to say to make a man feel good about himself. I appreciated the compliment anyway.

After we had finished, she looked at me and said, 'I'm starving. Brekky?'

I said to her, 'I feel as though I've just run a marathon!'

She laughed. 'Get used to it.'

As we both got up to go to the kitchen, I noticed a photo of a fella on her bedside table. I didn't notice it the night before because it had been dark. 'Who's the photo of?' I enquired.

'Oh, that's Paul. I'll tell you about him another time.'

'It he an ex?'

She looked at me and said, 'Sort of. We'll talk about him later.'

She obviously didn't want to talk about him so I dropped it. I didn't know it at the time, but I learned later that Jann was also in love with Paul. He was Jann's first sexual partner, but the funny thing was that he was gay and she knew it.

From the kitchen, I looked down at my unit and saw Leonard. I waved and he waved back. 'So this is how you see us from up here,' I said, laughing.

We had breakfast and a bit of a chat before I had to go. I had nothing to go to, I just didn't want to overstay. As I left her unit that morning, I came to a realisation that I had never thought possible: Jann was 'The One'. I mean, you hear them say it in movies a lot, but to actually feel it is surreal. I was generally a shy man and found it difficult to talk to women, but not Jann. Words flowed as easily as if I was talking to my best mate.

A week or so had passed and we'd been out to dinner at the Pine Inn at Burwood and a couple of other places. I loved the Pine Inn. It was a friendly tavern-type atmosphere. Cook your own steaks on the chargrill. A few drinks with friends. Very relaxed. A few more visits to her unit and a few to mine. If I look back on it, it was a typical progression for a relationship.

One Saturday, I was in Jann's kitchen doing the dishes and she walked in.

'I'm late,' she said in a worried voice.

I said, 'Where do you have to be?'

'No, I'm late. George hasn't come to visit.'

'Who's George?'

She just looked at me and tilted her head to the side slightly. I said, 'Oh, wow! What happens now?' all the time thinking to myself, *Why do you refer to your periods as 'George'?*

She said, 'I don't know. We just have to wait and see. What will you do if I am pregnant?'

I said, 'We could get married.'

That was the worst thing I could have said. I could see the look of horror on her face.

She said, 'I'm not getting married. I'm not ready. I won't have it.'

I said, 'Whatever you want to do, I'd support you.' I was actually thinking that I'd love to be a dad and I'd love to be married to Jann. What I also thought was, *Wow! Given her reaction to my answer, maybe she doesn't love me.* Neither of us had brought up the 'L' word before. Although I had been feeling it, I didn't want to rush her.

She made an appointment to see the doctor the next Wednesday. I drove her there but she didn't want me to come in, so I dropped her off and picked her up when she was done. She wasn't pregnant. She was so relieved. I was a bit sad, I suppose. The thought of becoming a dad was very appealing to me. It was probably for the best as far as Jann was concerned.

CHAPTER THREE

One Friday night, my brother rang and said he had tickets to 'The Hooters' who were playing at the Hordern Pavilion. I wanted to tell Jann but she wasn't home from university, so I went to the concert and had a good night out with my brother. We weren't that close so to get an invite from him was nice. After the gig, we went back to his place.

He was doing his thing with a friend of his. She was a 'really good sort'.

I was left in the lounge room with this other girl, not knowing what to do. She was older than I was. I wasn't going to cheat on Jann and that was that. It became awkward sitting there looking at each other, listening to the noises coming out of the other room, so I yelled out to Max, 'I'm going.'

'Yeah, no worries,' came the muffled reply from the bedroom.

I got home about 1.30 am and looked up. Jann's place was in darkness.

When I got up later in the morning, I looked up again to see if Jann was around. I saw her in the window of her kitchen. I waved but she didn't return the gesture. She saw me and turned away. That night out with my brother proved to be a turning point in my relationship with Jann. Not one that I was happy about.

Leonard and Scott returned from touch football. Scott was our new flatmate. We needed help to pay the rent. Leonard said, 'Ah, by the way, I think Jann has the shits with you.'

'Why?'

'Because you went out without telling her. I think she thinks you went out with another girl.'

I said, 'I wouldn't do that. Why would she think that?'

'Stuffed if I know,' he said, with a hint of guilt in his voice.

I went up to Jann's place and knocked on the door. There was no answer. I kept knocking but she wouldn't come to the door. I eventually went home. I kept looking up to her window and balcony hoping to catch a glimpse of her or Missy so that I could find out what was going on.

One night, I was looking up and saw two guys in her unit. It was then that I thought that maybe I had been just a fling and had been cast aside to make way for the new. I didn't know what else it could be. I saw her in the window and she saw me and waved as if to say, 'I can do it too'. She wasn't smiling at the time. I knew that something was terribly wrong.

To say that I was devastated would be the biggest understatement of all time. My head was spinning with so much confusion. I didn't sleep well that night.

The next morning, I cornered Missy out the front of her unit block at the bus stop. I said, 'Missy, what's going on with Jann?'

She said, 'What do you care?'

'What do you mean, what do I care? Of course I care; I'm in love with her.'

'Yeah, right. If you were in love, you wouldn't have gone out with some other girl without telling her.'

'I didn't go out with another girl,' I said.

She said, 'A week ago, you went out with another girl. Leonard and his mate told us.'

'I went out with my brother. We went to see 'The Hooters'. I didn't go out with another girl.'

'Well, it's too late now, she's found someone else.'

I said, 'Can you please get her to call me, Missy. I really want to sort this out.'

'I'll tell her, but I don't think she will speak with you.'

You could've stabbed me in the stomach with a knife and it would have actually relieved the pain I was feeling. I raced back down to my unit to see Leonard. He had gone to work. I sat there stewing for a while. I couldn't go to work so I phoned in sick. I spent the day at home in bed. I didn't know what to do. The love of my life had left me because of some bullshit that my so-called mate had spun. I have no idea what his motive was; however, I just don't think he liked to see me happy, considering that Missy had rejected him. What an absolute fuck.

A month after we had broken up, I received a letter from the NSW Police Service accepting my application to join them. It was the most exciting news I'd had in a while and really took my mind off Jann. At least for a short time. I was told in the letter to report to the NSW Police Academy in Goulburn on 26 September 1986.

I rang everybody I knew and told them the news. Everyone was over the moon. I even rang Jann who said, 'Well done, Mitch.' She then wished me well and hung up.

I rang her straight back. 'Hello,' came her familiar voice.

'Jann, it's me. Can we talk please?'

'What about? I don't think there's much to talk about do you?'

I said, 'Yes, I need to know what went wrong.'

'You hurt me. That's what went wrong,' she said.

I said, 'I'm coming up,' and hung up.

I was about halfway when I saw her walking towards me. She wasn't happy. She said, 'Sit!' She gestured to the concrete steps in the pathway.

We sat on the step where I explained the whole situation with Leonard and Scott telling lies. Obviously, Missy had not passed on my message. She told me that she was very hurt and that she couldn't see me anymore in case she got hurt again. She added that she still cared for me but only wanted to be friends. Again, devastation started to set in and I began to tear up, but then I realised that I could maintain the friendship and hopefully she could learn to love me as time went by. In the back of my mind though, I was thinking, *She's not trying very hard. If that's all it took to upset her, maybe it's for the best.* But I soon learned that that is not how I function. I had become very attached, as you do to the person you're in love with. I thought to myself that I was going to work at it because I loved her.

The weeks passed and we kept talking and were getting on fairly well. Jann told me that she was just about to finish university for the year and was heading home to Collarenebri. She asked me if I wanted to come up for a visit. I thought to myself, *This sounds promising.* She said she'd be at pony camp for the first week but any time after that was fine. I tried to phone her to let her know I was coming but, at that time, the phones in the bush were antiquated. It was still a matter of being connected by an operator. I tried phoning a couple of times but no one answered Eventually, I gave up and decided to go for a nice little drive anyway.

Jann had been gone for about a week and, in the meantime, I had been busy with work and organising a hire car to go and see her. I headed up to Collarenebri, which was an eight-hour drive from Croydon Park. I got up for an early start and drove continuously, only stopping for petrol.

The landmarks given by Jann were fairly abstract but I followed them to the letter. You know, turn right at the big tree which is fifteen kilometres past the last light post. That sort of thing. I got to the final mark – the crooked street sign. I turned left and then I saw the gate sign to 'Paterson Station'. I arrived at about two in the afternoon. I drove in the gate and up to the Queenslander-style house. There were large green trees around the house, two large sheds out the back, and a couple of dogs – a typical farm setting. I got out of the car and noticed the dry heat. I liked it; no humidity. I parked, locked the car, as you do in the city out of habit, and knocked on the door.

A lady came to the door. 'Hello,' she said, in the typically friendly tone you would expect of a farmer's wife.

I said, 'Hi. Is Jann here please?'

'No, she's at pony club and won't be back until later this afternoon.'

'I'm Mitch, her friend from Sydney. She invited me up for the weekend.'

'Hi Mitch, I'm Judy,' she said, with a smile. 'She didn't mention to me that you were coming but that's not unusual for Jann. Would you like a drink?'

'I'd love one. That would be great. Thank you.' I sat and drank a large glass of water as Judy excused herself to continue baking in the kitchen. Whatever she was baking, it smelt fantastic.

Several hours passed, when I heard the sound of a car coming up the driveway. I walked around the veranda and saw a four-wheel drive with Jann in the passenger seat and her brother, Allan, driving. He pulled up in front of the house, which was around the back. I walked up to her and said, 'Hi, how are you?'

She said, 'Hello, what are you doing here?' in a surprised, but seemingly happy, voice.

'You invited me, remember?'

'No, but that doesn't matter. You're here now, that's the main thing.' She started telling me about pony club and what she'd been doing there. Then she said that she was going to show me around.

We jumped into this old land rover and she started to show me around the property. It seemed to go forever. I said, 'How big is this place?'

'32,000 acres' she said.

Wow! That's a lot of land I thought. We were out for about an hour and hadn't scratched the surface.

I saw Jann look at her watch. She exclaimed, 'Shit, we've got to head back, I've arranged to meet some friends in at the Tattersalls Hotel in Colli. You can come if you like, or you can stay here.'

I'd travelled all that way to see Jann, why would I stay with her parents. 'No, I'll come' I said.

We drove back to the house, had a shower, and got dressed ready to go out. We arrived at the hotel just after dark and, as soon as we got there, Jann ran to meet her friends. She introduced me to them; however, I felt as though I wasn't meant to be there so I just sat and listened.

Jann ignored me for the whole night. If I had got up and left, I'm sure she wouldn't have known I was gone. I know they were friends she had known for a long time, but I was a little pissed off I have to say. I suppose that's why she asked if I wanted to stay at the house.

A few things started to make me think about what I was doing. Maybe when she said 'friends', she really did mean 'friends'. Maybe I had read too much into the invitation to come up. Maybe I was a play toy to keep her occupied until she had something, or somebody, more interesting to play with.

It was getting late and I was stuffed from the drive up from Sydney. I was falling asleep on my bar stool. Finally, she asked me if I wanted to go. She apologised for ignoring me but that was cold comfort. The drive back to the homestead was very quiet. Unnervingly so, in fact. We were about two-thirds of the way back when Jann said, 'Pull over.'

I said, 'Pardon?'

'Pull over, we need to talk!' she exclaimed.

I stopped the car in the middle of the road because I didn't want to get bogged in the sometimes soggy table drains.

Jann said, 'Why did you come out here?'

'Because you invited me.'

'But why really?'

'Because I'm in love with you.'

She said, 'No, Mitch, you don't want to love someone like me. I'll only hurt you. Look what happened back at the pub. I ignored you all night. People in love don't do that to each other.'

'So you don't love me?'

'No, I don't,' she said. 'I care about you a lot and I still want to be friends but that's all it can be.'

It was all I could do to stop myself from breaking down in front of her, but I kept it together. 'So should I leave tomorrow morning then?'

She said, 'No. Stay tomorrow and you can leave the next morning. That way, you'll be fresh for the drive home. I'll be back in Sydney in a couple of weeks. We can talk more then.'

'Is there anything left to talk about?' I asked.

'You never know,' she replied. She looked at me and put her hand on my cheek to comfort me. 'You're a wonderful man, Mitch. There's someone out there who's right for you. I just don't think it's me.' She could see how upset I was.

I started the car and continued the drive back to Peterson. One of the worst things about that conversation was that I had 'Fleetwood Mac' playing in the cassette player at the time. Now, whenever I hear 'Song Birds', I have a flashback to that night.

The next day, we went for another drive and just hung out. That's what I came up here for – to hang out with her without any distractions. We took a rifle because she knew I liked to shoot. The first thing she told me was not to shoot a female roo. The first thing I did ... I shot a female roo. It was unintentional. I didn't know how to tell the difference. It had a joey in the pouch which jumped out when mum hit the ground. I chased it and caught it and picked it up.

Jann said, 'Dad's going to be really upset with you.'

'Why?'

'Because there aren't any wildlife services around here and he's the one who'll have to hit it over the head.'

We took it back to the house because I couldn't do it. Jann was right. David wasn't happy. He said in a gruff voice, 'I told you not to shoot any females. Now I have to get rid of it.' I apologised to him but he was still upset with me.

By dinner that night, it had been forgotten, which I appreciated. After dinner, we all sat down at the kitchen table and they taught me how to play cards. It was a fun night with plenty of laughs and I was made to feel right at home. It was me and Allan against Jann and Judy. I had a lot of beginners' luck but the girls piped us at the post. When it was bedtime, I took Jann to her room and we had a bit of a chat before I went to my room and lay there thinking about what might have been. I didn't sleep much that night.

The following morning, I got up early and left before Jann got up. I knew it would upset me more to see her before I headed off, so I thanked David and Judy for their hospitality and left. I knew she'd be back in Sydney before too long but I didn't want to say goodbye to her. My emotions were still running high.

I shed many tears on the way back to Sydney. The funny thing was that, even though she had told me she wasn't romantically interested in me anymore, I still thought I could make her fall in love with me again. I didn't think it was beyond me.

On the way back to Sydney, I stopped at Taree to talk to Ron and Valerie. I had known Ron and Valerie for the majority of my life and they were like my second parents. I told them what had happened and totally lost it. Valerie comforted me and Ron quoted the most irritating line in the history of relationships: 'There are plenty more ...' Yes,

I know you know how that ends. Nobody in my position ever wants to hear those words spoken in this situation ... ever. What makes that saying worse is that I truly believe that every person alive has one person who is the 'One' for them. My 'One' is Jann.

I had lunch with Ron and Valerie and continued my drive back to Sydney. I was actually glad to get back home. Leonard's constant stupidity took my mind off Jann for short periods of time. However, it was hard, knowing that every time I looked out of the lounge room window, the reminder was there.

CHAPTER FOUR

Leonard, Clint, and I went out on the town the night I got back. I didn't drink much normally; however, it was one of the few times in my life when I drank so much that I wasn't in control of rational thought. We were at the Rocks and looking up at the Sydney Harbour Bridge.

Leonard said, 'What about it?'

I said, 'Shit yeah,' knowing exactly what he was talking about.

Clint looked a bit bewildered wondering what we were on about.

We started walking up under the bridge and climbing the pylon. Clint said, 'Fuck that! I'm not goin' up there.'

I said, 'No worries, yell out if you see any cops.'

Leonard and I proceeded to climb the bridge. This was well before it became fashionable to do so (after paying way too much for the privilege). We had to climb around the spiked safety devices at the bottom of the stairs to the lower arch. That meant one slip and we were dead meat. We successfully negotiated this meager attempt to keep such intrepid explorers at bay. From here on in, it was easy going to the top of the lower arch of the bridge.

Once at the top, we sat and enjoyed the view. Leonard pulled his last stubby out of his pants and offered me a drink. I passed. We yelled down to Clint, who was still waiting at the bottom. Probably wasn't the best idea as we attracted the attention of other passersby as well ... luckily, no cops.

We both looked up and looked at each other at the same time. We knew there was a bigger challenge to be had. We began the slow and arduous climb up the steel girder. It was a terrifying climb but a climb that we felt had to be made. Only the thought of climbing to greatness would help me to put the thought of not being with Jann behind me for good. An hour after we started (and around 3.30 am that Sunday morning), we reached the top of the grandest coat hanger on earth.

The breeze was warm and steady. We could hear the sound of the Australian and New South Wales flags fluttering above us up their respective flagpoles. We watched as the cars below whizzed silently beneath us, the only sound being the 'click click, click click, click click' as they crossed the expansion joints of the road surface. I sat and watched as Leonard climbed the flagpole and touched the very top to claim the ultimate bragging rights to this magnificent feat we'd accomplished. I felt like we were the first to achieve this goal. Is this what Sir Edmund Hillary felt like when he conquered Mount Everest? I think so, although, I doubt he was pissed when he did it. Plus, he had a heap of people helping him with a lot of climbing gear ... pussy!

We were the true heroes of the night. We sat for a while and pondered life and the quiet city below before we made our way down the long stairway of the upper arch towards the bottom of the bridge. The climb back over the spikey fence was more terrifying than on the way up because we knew we were almost home and didn't want to fall at the last hurdle. Finally, setting foot firmly back on terra firma, we gave each other a hug and then we looked for Clint. There he was, curled up on the park bench ... asleep. We woke him and decided to head for home. The sun was just starting to come up and, to tell you the truth, I was knackered. We all were.

The next day, Thomas came down to visit again. Whenever he came down, we always had a lot of fun. This time, we went for a drive in the Subie and had nothing to do. We saw a motorbike in the backyard of a house which backed onto a lane. Well, it was too enticing for Thomas, so he hotwired it and we took turns riding it around Sydney. We ended up riding it all the way over to Belmore. I was driving the Subie and Thomas was on the bike.

We were in the middle of the road talking when a police car came around the corner. Thomas took off on the bike and I just sat there as the police pulled up to talk to us.

'What's going on boys?' the policeman asked.

I told him that the bloke on the bike was lost and was asking directions. He was happy with that and drove off. Leonard and I were happy with the result but Clint was shitting himself. He was funny to go out with. At the end of the night, we left the bike parked nicely on the side of the road. The Subie, on the other hand, had to go. We found a nice little cul-de-sac and torched the sucker. That car had been through way too much for us to hang onto her any more. It wasn't insured and it wasn't registered in my name. I figured the worse we could get done for was littering. We lit it up and hung around just long enough to get a couple of good Polaroids of it for the last time, and then we went home.

When we got home early that morning, we all went to bed. When I got up later that day, I went out and bought a HK Holden for a hundred and fifty bucks. To celebrate, that night Clint, Leonard, and I took the HK up to Kings Cross for the night. I had this favourite joke I used to like to play on the motoring public. On the way up to the Cross, we'd fake a break-down and stop the car in the middle of the road and lift the bonnet. The traffic would bank back for kilometres while we just sat there until the tow truck came. Miraculously, when the tow truck arrived, the car would start. Then it was business as usual and off to the strip clubs. On those nights out, the night usually blended into the next day. There was too much living to be had for a few boys from the bush. There were many mornings to spend watching the sun come up from North Head.

After our night out at the Cross, the only thing different for me was that I immediately began to reflect on what I had done the previous night and where I was heading. Six months from now and I would have to lock myself up.

As time went on, I spoke to Jann frequently; almost every day, in fact. I saw different men come and go and, to tell you the truth, it hurt like hell. I don't know if it was jealousy or envy; probably a bit of both. I thought as time went by the hurt would lessen. It never did.

I was riding my bike to work one morning when a car turned left in front of me. I had nowhere to go so I slammed into the side of the car. The impact threw me over the bonnet and onto the road. I had a bad cut on my knee and 'bark' off me everywhere. The front wheel of my bike was bent at right angles and so I was stranded. I borrowed a phone belonging to one of the shopkeepers who came to help to phone work to tell them what had happened; however, they were most unsympathetic. I told them that I would be having a few days off work and they told me that if I wasn't at work the next day, to not bother coming back. That was on the Monday. On the Thursday, I arrived at work and was taken into the office. Vince, the operations manager, said simply, 'Mitch, you don't work here anymore.' I told him I was in an accident and showed him all of the scars from the stitches and grazes. He didn't want to know. I had only been there twelve months and really loved that job. It was the first time I had been sacked. It didn't feel good at all.

I was out of work for a week or so when a friend of the family offered me a job at the Bankstown RSL Club. I was about to head off for my first shift when Leonard told me he was throwing a party at home that night. I thought to myself, *When Leonard has a party, they are usually events to remember.* But I had to work. I turned up to work and started my first shift, which was to pick up glasses and put them in the washing machine and that sort of thing. It was as boring as bat shit so, at 11.30 pm, I faked a stomach-ache.

The boss said, 'You've only been here since 8.00 pm. If you leave now, don't come back.'

I thought for all of one second and said, 'See ya,' and left.

When I got back to our unit, I knew it was the best decision I had made in the last forty-five minutes. It was a two-bedroom unit and there were about eighty people there. Some of the shit that went on that night was downright disgusting but I wouldn't have missed it. Needless to say, I didn't get any more offers of work from family friends.

Losing my job at George Hudson made me really despondent and more determined than ever to join the police force. I didn't know when that would be, so I applied for a job as a data entry clerk in the actuaries department at Prudential Assurance in Martin Place and got it. The people there were really nice and showed me exactly what to do. I had no experience but had taught myself to type as part of my preparation to enter the police force. This was a valuable skill, as that was what I did ... ALL DAY – enter data into the computer. Surprisingly, I liked the job more than I'd thought I would. No stress, the people were great, and I loved working in the city. I used to have lunch in Martin Place and either have a sleep in the sun or watch the street performers strut their stuff.

I got home one afternoon and collected the mail. There was a letter there from the police force. It confirmed that I had been accepted into the NSW Police Force and that my start date was 26 September 1986. I had barely been at Prudential for a month. When I spoke to Julie, my boss, she was very upset that she was losing me: not because I had only been there for a month, but she said she really liked me and loved my work ethic, plus I got along with everyone in the office. She sat me down and tried to convince me to stay, but I couldn't. I had a path which I needed to follow. I gave her a week's notice. She wished me well and I left.

It was at that point in my life that I decided that enough was enough. My skylarking days were over. I suppose I had always been looking for approval from the people I thought cared about me. My insecurities were real and I would do anything to be accepted. I don't know what the real answer is as to why I did the things I did. Maybe it's just the way I'm wired. Some people murder, some people commit armed robberies; I knock over phone boxes and climb bridges. I just don't know why.

Around came 25 September 1986 – the day before I moved down to the Police Academy. I was as nervous as all get out. I packed everything and went up to see Jann. We hung out all day and had a great time. We went to dinner at the restaurant up in Sydney Tower. It was wonderful. The photo of us together at Sydney Tower is the only photo I have of Jann and I love it. On the way home, I bought her a big bunch of flowers and a card. I wrote in it: 'To my darling Jann. Thank you for being you. All my love, Mitch'. She read the card and gave me a hug. She looked at me with those gorgeous eyes and kissed me. I knew it was a 'thank you' kiss and not anything more, but it was so nice.

We hung out some more, just around her flat. By this time, it was well into the night. I got up to go home but, before I could take a step, Jann kissed me again. This was no 'thank you' kiss.

'You want to stay the night?' she whispered in my ear.

I nodded and we went into her bedroom and went to bed. We made love for an hour and a half. It was the most intense session we had ever had. She cuddled up to me and I just lay there all night, not sleeping a wink. I had to be down at the academy by 2.00 pm. I had to go. I slid my arm out from under her beautiful head, kissed her on the forehead, and left.

My stint at the Police Academy was to last for three months. It was very exciting and enlightening. I passed every exam with flying colours and was in the top five per cent of my class of 220 trainees. During the course, I travelled home every weekend. The first weekend was to find that Leonard was moving out to a flat closer to his work, near Blacktown. With no notice, I had a bit of a panic attack because I knew I couldn't afford to pay the rent on my own.

A friend of mine from Year 12, who was living out at Ingleburn, phoned to say hello. Connor Dwyer was his name, but I called him CID because they were his initials. 'I' for Ian. He was one of my best mates at school. He was telling me about his new job with Jetset Travel in North Sydney and how the travelling was killing him. I asked him if he would like to move in with me. He jumped at the chance and so it was a done deal.

It's amazing how you can be such good friends until you live together. Conner was a great bloke. Loved his music, hated cleaning up after himself. He used to leave his dirty socks around the lounge room, which really pissed me off. It's just as easy to throw them in your room or, better still, in the laundry basket. He used to laugh and say that if he was an officer in the German army during the Second World War, he would have been called, 'Heir Dwyer'. We thought it was funny.

I was nearing the end of my training and I was so excited that I was finally going to become a police officer. It was kind of ironic really, considering what I got up to as a kid and, to a large extent, recently. One way or another, I thought I was destined to be looking at iron bars. I thought it would be best to look at them from the outside of the cell.

About a week out from final exams, I decided to ring Jann and ask her to wish me luck and to plan something for when I came home. Missy answered the phone.

'Hello,' came the greeting in her usual jovial voice.

'Hi, Missy, it's me. Is Jann there please?' There was a pause, and I could hear muffled voices as Missy covered the mouth piece of the phone. 'Ah ... she is, but she's occupied at the moment.'

I said, 'I can hear her in the background. What's she doing?'

'She's got company,' came the reply.

'Can you put her on please?'

'She doesn't want to talk to you.'

'Why not?'

'Look Mitch,' Missy said, in a now impatient voice. 'She doesn't want to see you anymore. She's going out with someone else.' She hung up the phone.

I immediately rang back.

Someone picked up the phone. 'Hello,' I said. No answer. 'Hello,' I said again. I could hear giggling in the background which I knew was Missy. 'Jann?'

A male voice said, 'She doesn't wanna talk to you mate, so don't call her, ok?' He then hung up.

At that point, I would have done anything to be able to flick a switch to make the pain go away. I was sitting at my desk in my room at the Police Academy studying for my final exams. Yeah right ... not much study got done. I went and sat in the normally bustling common room and watched TV alone. Everyone else was doing what I should have been doing. Final exams started the next day. Shit!

The exams came and went over the next couple of days, and then came the agonizing wait to see how I'd done. We had to wait until Monday morning. It was a restless weekend for everyone. We went out to the Taralgon Hotel to let our hair down. It was a very big night. There were 213 future police officers in the one hotel drinking as much as we could to relieve the stressful experience of exams, and celebrating the end of our training. These results would determine our future.

Monday morning rolled around soon enough. All recruits filed into the main auditorium for the moment of truth. The superintendent of the academy took his place at the lectern. 'Quiet please, everyone. Quiet please. Settle down.' Slowly, the incoherent sound of 213 voices dimmed as the hall finally fell silent. 'As you know,' he continued, 'the results I am about to hand you will determine two things: whether you've passed the course and your seniority in relation to your other classmates. If your name isn't called, you will be required to re-sit the exams because you have failed to make the grade. Please come down to the front, follow Sergeant Smith, and he will explain what you need to do.'

He started to read the names in alphabetical order. I had been in the top five per cent of the class the whole time, so I was looking on with interest to see who wasn't pulling their weight. Suddenly, I noticed that he had bypassed the 'W's' without calling my name. All of my friends looked at me. I was absolutely shitting myself. Could the stress of being unceremoniously dumped by Jann have caused me to falter at the last hurdle?

I made my way with Sergeant Smith, and several other recruits to the Superintendent's office where we all sat waiting until he had finished handing out the rest of the results. I couldn't believe I had missed getting my results in front of all my mates, and witnessed them and their smiles as they received theirs. It took quite a while but, eventually, the super came into the office. There were five people who had failed the exams. He started to explain the process to re-sit the exam.

I said, 'Excuse me, Sir.'

'Yes?' he said.

'Sir, my name is Mitchell Walton and I was wondering if you could check my results. I have been doing well the whole time. I didn't think I would fail. There are two of us with the same name. Did we both fail?'

He replied, 'Oh, ok. I'll check for you.' There was a short pause. 'Let me see ... What's your name again? Mitchell wasn't it?'

'Yes, Sir,' I replied.

He looked up at me with his dry expression. This guy never smiled. He said, 'Mitchell, you not only passed, but you came equal second in the exam and tenth overall. Congratulations. You can go.'

'Thank you, Sir,' I said with relief, knowing that the guy next to me had to re-sit his failed subjects.

I left the office and ran to the common room where I could hear everyone celebrating. As I walked through the doors, the common room went quiet.

Tucky said, 'What happened?'

'It wasn't me, it was Rusty.'

Everyone was so happy for me and we just sat around as the realisation that we had made it began to sink in. There were only two things still left: to find out where we would be posted and the passing-out parade.

I rang Jann to tell her what was happening. We were having a nice chat when she suddenly said, 'I'm going up to Mum and Dad's for a break. Pete is going to sea. Would you be able to look after his car until we get back?' What a weird thing to ask: for your ex-boyfriend to look after your new boyfriend's car.

'No worries,' I said.

'We are moving to a new place in Stanmore when we get back, so when I get settled in we'll have to catch up.' All I could think of was that she was not going to be close to me anymore. That was probably a good thing, because her living so close was a constant source of pain.

I drove Pete's car around for a couple of weeks because it was a V8 and had a full tank of petrol. I finally got tired of looking after it though, so I left it out the front in Milton Street, Ashfield, with the driver's window down a smidgen. As planned, it was gone the next morning. They found it burnt out over at Canterbury. My mate, Paffy, took a photo of me doing a massive burn out in it though. Great shot!

The upside of Jann moving was that Chris and I got to move into a better unit ... Jann's unit. Obviously, I took the room that contained so many memories for me with the love of my life.

Now that the formalities of training were over, we could relax a little. The fitness class was now optional. There was a recruits versus instructors soccer game. Instructors won because they played dirty. In a fun way though. But there was still the dreaded curfew. We had to be in by 10.00 pm each night.

The next day, our posting came out. We were allowed three preferences of station. I chose Kings Cross, Central, and Ballina. I got none. I got posted to Flemington – 32nd Division, otherwise known as 'the retirement home' because nothing ever happens there. Needless to say, I was disappointed big time.

The following day was our passing-out parade. My family and some friends had travelled down to Goulburn to watch as I took my oath to serve the people of New South Wales in the protection of life and property. The night before, I had been out to dinner with Mum and Dad. I was getting pretty nervous. I said my goodbyes to them in their motel room and went back to my room at the academy. At 4.00 am, I was awoken by an almighty banging on my door.

'Fuck off!' I yelled.

A voice came from the other side. 'It's Sergeant Jason. Open the door.'

I jumped out of bed and opened the door. I said, 'Sorry, Sarge. What's up?'

He said, 'Where have you been?'

'I went out to dinner with my parents.'

'What time did you arrive back?'

I immediately thought, *Shit! I forgot to sign back in.* 'I forgot to sign in, didn't I?'

'Yes, you did, and now I have to run around chasing you up. You're almost a police officer, Walton. That means you have to display a level of responsibility to yourself and the community.'

I said, 'Am I in the shit?'

He said, 'Not this time, but I want a report on my desk first thing in the morning explaining why you were late. Good night.'

I shut the door and went back to sleep.

It was 19 December 1986 and Recruit Class 223 was about to graduate. I woke up at 7.30 am. Everyone else had already been up for an hour. We had breakfast, got showered, ironed our uniforms, got dressed, and went up to get issued with our appointments belt, which included our Smith & Wesson .38 caliber revolver. We also had a final rehearsal for the parade, which we had spent many hours practicing already. One bit of controversy spreading like wildfire was that two cadets had been sacked overnight for 'getting it on' down on the footy field. Apart from the curfew, that was the other biggy ... No Bonking Your Mates. It must have been very embarrassing for the family when they arrived. Unfortunately, he had to tell his wife why he was dismissed the night before he was due to graduate. She was single so it was only Mum and Dad she had to tell.

Anyway, the passing out parade went well, save for a couple of recruits who couldn't handle the heat and fainted. *Wimps!* I thought. After the superintendent's speech, we were dismissed. We turned to the left, took three paces, and 206 newly-appointed police officers threw their hats high into the air. The smart ones wrote their names on the inside. The not-so-smart ones looked like idiots as they were trying on each other's hats to find one that would fit. These are the people who have sworn their allegiance to protect the community. Not to worry. In the end, 220 had started, two were dismissed, five had to re-sit their exams, and seven dropped out.

CHAPTER FIVE

I made my way back to my flat. I walked in the front door and Connor was sitting on the lounge. He just laughed. Considering what we used to get up to together, it must have been a stretch for him to think of me as a cop. I didn't know what he was thinking. Gee it's funny to see Mitch in a cop uniform, where's the fancy dress party or, shit, can I still smoke my weed and not get busted?

On 23 December 1986 at 6.45 am, I attended Flemington Police Station for my very first shift. My best mate from the academy, Tucky, also got stationed there, so at least there was a familiar face.

My first job in the police force was attending a motor vehicle accident between a Repco delivery driver and a taxi. The delivery driver wasn't too bad-looking. I didn't even have to muster the courage to ask her for her phone number because it was part of the job. How good was this? A few days after the accident, I rang her from work under the guise of getting more information about the accident. I eventually asked her if she wanted to go out sometime. After telling me she hated cops, she told me I seemed different and she agreed. Her name was Janette.

We only went out three or four times. I wasn't really into her and she never put out, so I just stopped calling her. She tried leaving messages at work, but I told her I was being transferred and that I couldn't see her anymore. Worked a treat. I've always said honesty is the best policy. I didn't say when I was being transferred so, technically, I wasn't lying.

I was rostered on station duty and was sitting at my desk minding my own business when the phone rang. I picked up the phone and answered, 'Flemington Police Station.'

The voice on the other end came at me like a freight train. 'Who is that man?'

'My name is Constable Walton, Sir.'

'Then that's the way I want the phone answered. Do you understand?'

I asked the voice on the end of the phone, 'Can I help you, Sir?'

He said, 'This is Assistant Commissioner Blunt. Put me through to the officer in charge.'

'Right away, Sir,' I replied.

At that stage, they had changed the name from the 'police force' to the 'police service'. There was a big push on for police to be seen less as thugs with authority and more as public servants. As far as I'm concerned that was the beginning of the end.

The most intriguing thing about being a police officer at Flemington and, I suppose, anywhere else really, was the acceptance of corruption. It was on a very minor scale at Flemington compared to other locations, but it was still prevalent. I remember this one particular sergeant I was on patrol with. He said he wanted to try on some shoes so we went into a shoe shop. He sat down and tried on some black leather dress shoes. He had a walk around and told the shoe salesman that he'd take them. He removed them so that the salesman could put them back in the box. He then walked out of the shop with the shoe box under his arm. When he said he'd take them, I didn't think he meant literally. The shopkeeper looked at me. I didn't know what to do. I just left and kept my mouth shut.

The other quirky thing that used to go on was that, every Friday morning, the junior constables – meaning me or one of the other probationers – would have to jump in the paddy wagon and drive around to the various stalls at the markets and fill the back of the truck with fruit and veg. It was supposed to be an unwritten contract for expedient investigation should there be a crime committed against one of the stallholders. That paddy wagon was so full we'd have to jam the door shut. We would then drive back to the station and the fruit and veg would be distributed in order of rank. Chief inspectors got first choice, inspectors next, sergeants, and so on, until the probationers got what little there was left. It didn't take long before I began to drive from the markets to my house and then back to the station. Nobody was ever any the wiser. Premium quality fruit for the next twelve months.

Domestic violence was a big problem in the Auburn patrol and sometimes we were called upon to work that patrol when Flemington was quiet, which was most of the time. This one night, I was working with a new recruit who was doing his first nightshift – Probationary Constable Darren. We were called to a domestic dispute in Park Road, Auburn. On attending the victim's address, I could see that she was terribly upset and distressed. I asked where the husband (offender) was and she told me he was next door. I asked Constable Darren to look after the victim while I went and spoke to the offender.

I would have only been five minutes with the offender but, when I returned to the front door of the victim's house,

I looked straight down the hallway and spotted Constable Darren standing there with his pants around his boots and the victim giving him what could only be described as a happy ending.

The very next night, the woman came to the police station to give a statement. Constable Darren took her into the sergeant's office and gave it to her on the desk. It made me wonder why this man and his wife were having domestic problems. Then I thought to myself, *Who am I to judge? I'm just there to make sure he doesn't beat the crap out of her or the other way around*, as has happened on occasion.

* * * *

Over that twelve-month period, Jann was never far from my thoughts. When I was on night work and she was the page eight Sister at Royal Prince Alfred Hospital, we use to chat every now and again, but the chats became fewer and further between.

Towards the end of my probationary period, an opportunity came up for me to transfer to the country. By now, I had realised that Jann had moved on and that there was nothing keeping me in Sydney. Walgett was the only station on offer. I had camped out there as a young fella and had a fondness for the outback. I put in my transfer papers and was successful. My patrol commander nearly had a conniption. I think I was his golden child and he didn't want me to go. In fact, he told me he was going to do everything he could to keep me from going. It was flattering, but I explained to him why I had to go. He reluctantly allowed my transfer to proceed.

CHAPTER SIX

In December 1987, I moved to Walgett. On my first night in Walgett, I went to the RSL for dinner. I phoned my mum to say, 'Hi'. I guess I just wanted to hear a familiar voice. *It's going to be a lonely two years*, I thought to myself as I hung up the phone. It wasn't really.

As I was standing at the bar, one of the coppers came up and introduced me to a few of the locals. Cherie was the first girl he introduced me to but with a caveat. 'Don't bother,' he said. 'Unless you're going to marry her, you ain't gotta chance.' She was from outside of Wauchope on the Mid North Coast of New South Wales. My neck of the woods. We were friends but, as he said, no chance.

I was listening to a couple of locals chatting at the bar. There were three topics of conversation in Walgett: stock condition and pricing, the weather, and the weekend cricket. Not much else. The only thing that changed really was the sport, depending on the season.

My very first shift at Walgett was spent looking around the township, getting my bearings, and so on. After lunch, I was standing at the counter when the phone rang. I picked up the phone, 'Walgett Police Station.'

This voice came booming down the phone into my ear. 'Who is that man?'

I instantly recognised the voice from twelve months earlier – Assistant Commissioner Blunt. I thought to myself,

No – it can't be. I thought someone was playing a trick on me. I said, 'It's Constable Walton, Sir'.

He said, 'I've spoken to you about the manner in which you answer the phone before haven't I?'

I thought, *Fuck me! This bloke's good.* So, I simply said 'No, Sir – wasn't me. You must have been speaking to someone else. How can I help you?'

'Put me through to your Patrol Commander.' he blurted.

That taught me a new lesson that most people would have learned in primary school. Learn from your mistakes the first time. It makes life so much more comfortable.

Walgett is in the northwest of New South Wales. It's a very dry place. You can sit on the bonnet of your car and just take in the nothingness as the sun sets over the dusty western horizon. It is, however, a beautiful kind of nothingness. You can see lightning in the distance, but hear no thunder. You can smell the rain and the storm clouds would roll in, yet no rain falls. The rain was there, but for another day or another area. Walgett would miss out again.

One of the anomalies I couldn't get my head around the first time I saw it was the flooding. There was a dry spell that lasted for months. No sign of rain on the horizon. The skies would be blue and cloudless, yet before you could blink, the riverbanks would have broken and the area would be in flood. When it rained heavily in Queensland, the waters would flow down through the river system.

The two rivers that meet in Walgett are the Barwon and the Namoi Rivers. When they backed up, we were basically turned into an island. The township of Walgett is protected by a man-made levy bank surrounding the town so, while the town is spared, nobody gets in or out during a major flood. Even after the floodwaters subside, the black soil surrounding Walgett and the region in general has to dry out before you can drive on it. Some of the coppers used to live out of town on a property called 'Trilby Park'. Whenever it flooded they couldn't get to work, so the rest of us had to pick up the slack for them.

On the odd occasion that it did rain, if you were rostered for station duty, all you'd do all shift was to answer phone calls from people from the city wanting to know if the road from Walgett to Brewarrina was open or closed. This is the way a typical phone conversation would go:

Me: Walgett Police, Constable Walton speaking.

Dick Head: Hi mate, I was just wondering if the road from Walgett to Bree is open.

Me: No mate, it's shut.

Dick Head: I'm thinking of coming up tomorrow. Will it be open by then?

Me: No mate, it's an absolute bog hole. It's shut.

Dick Head: But I'm a good driver. I've been out there before.

Me: Sir, the road is closed for a reason. There is nothing getting through.

Dick Head: But I'm driving a Commodore.

Me: Hang up. Beep, beep, beep, beep.

The next afternoon:

Me: Walgett Police, Constable Walton speaking.

Dick Head: Hi mate, I've just tried to get to Bree on the Bree Road and I'm bogged. Can you help us out?

Me: I'll get the car crew to come out. How far did you make it?

Dick Head: Five k's past the levy.

Me: What type of car are you driving?

Dick Head: A Holden Commodore.

Me: You rang up yesterday to check the road condition, didn't you?

Dick Head: Er ... ah ... click. Beep, beep, beep.

I took up residence in 'The Barracks': a shared house owned by the police department which provided cheap accommodation for police who didn't mind sharing. Twenty-five dollars per week. Cheering! After I completed my move and my belongings had arrived, I settled into a new lifestyle; a relaxed lifestyle; one that I was more at home with.

I loved the countryside, and the locals were generally friendly. It was a relatively itinerant community with various employees from all government agencies there for a specific tenure and then they would move on. Preferably to a town more conducive to a better life style. Bankers, ambos, firies, teachers, nurses, and, of course, police. We all got on, both at work and after. You made it your business to know everyone else. You became friends with the ambos, firies, and nurses because you never knew when you might need them on your side. You didn't really need the teachers or the bankers, but they were usually a good source of sexual entertainment ... or so I heard.

* * * *

On my first afternoon shift at Walgett, which went from 3.00 pm until 11.00 pm, I got called to a motor vehicle accident on the Collarenebri Road. It was about three kilometres out of town. As I approached the collision site, I noticed that there was nobody in sight. What I did see troubled me deeply. Nothing could have prepared me for the carnage I was about to encounter.

I saw bodies all over the road. I saw a Subaru Brumby off to the side of the road on the left. I couldn't see any other vehicles. I did a body count and was stunned to find thirty-two dead or dying. There were piles of intestines on the roadway. Even an unborn fetus lay on the road next to the mother. There were even intestines caught in the bull bar of the Brumby and under the door handle of the car. I could hear what could be best described as bloodcurdling screams and moaning. I illuminated the roadway with the high beam and the spotlights of the police vehicle in order to help me locate the injured.

After calling it in to the station, I decided that I couldn't wait until help arrived. I had to take whatever action I needed to in order to alleviate the pain and suffering of those still alive and those who were mortally injured.

I made the decision and removed my .38 caliber Smith & Wesson revolver and made my way to the first of the injured. I pointed my firearm at a point directly between her eyes and fired. I had to perform this task on seven other sheep to end their pain. The final count was twenty four killed instantly, and eight that survived the impact but had to be put down.

After the fire brigade hosed the mess off the road, I drove to the Imperial Hotel in Walgett where I located the owner of the car at the bar, drinking. His version regarding what had happened: 'I fell asleep at the wheel.' Apparently, he had only gone to the pub to calm his nerves. Police are not idiots. We didn't come down in the last shower. A twelve-month suspension for DUI – not nearly enough considering the cruelty that he'd inflicted on those sheep, but better than nothing.

* * * *

About a week after I arrived, two other transferees turned up to the barracks – Stuart and Geoff – both out of my academy class. Stuart was very much a ladies' man and had no trouble 'picking up' in Walgett. I'm pretty sure he must have caught something at some stage. Nobody could have that much action and not catch something. Geoff was the same but to a lesser extent.

Great personalities both of them and all-round good fellas. You could always tell when Geoff had company in his room because he would have John Williamson's 'Crocodile Roll' playing on the cassette player. It was his signal to us that he was 'busy'. Stuart and Geoff were as thick as thieves and went everywhere together. They worked together, played together, and partied hard together. They were always whining about being in Walgett. My transfer was a request. They were forced to go. But for two guys who didn't want to be there they certainly made the best of what they had and who they had.

I'll never forget one period when Stuart was bangin' Sergeant Barnett's daughter. He was hell-bent on not letting Barnett find out. It was comical watching him trying to avoid Barnett and the conversations surrounding his daughter's whereabouts. Sweet little thing she was ... NOT. I know one thing for sure, she really loved her sex. The walls were thin in the barracks. We certainly knew how to party hard in Walgett.

Stuart and I went shooting one afternoon out on a property. We were walking through the long grass hunting wild pigs. We heard a rustle in the grass but I couldn't see what it was. The next thing, Stuart just shot from the hip. Baaaaaa. Baaaaaa. We looked at each other and Stuart wandered into the grass.

I said, 'Is it bad?'

'Well, if tripping over your own liver is bad, it's bad.' He then finished it off.

Even though the theory is that you never fire until you've identified your target, it's not until you actually do it that the theory sinks in. It's never happened since.

A month later, I had the opportunity of a lifetime: to lock up one of my former high school teachers for drink-driving. I pulled him over and submitted him to a roadside breath test. He was over the limit but, for some reason, I just couldn't do it. I told him this was his lucky day and to go straight home. There was no 'thank you', no nothing. I was kicking myself as he drove off. He was one cruel prick and I should have cashed in on my only opportunity to ping him.

Back when I was in high school, I had fallen asleep on the beach one Sunday and got burnt so badly, I thought I was a pig on a spit. My back just turned into one big blister. You know how it is – your skin contracts and gets tight so you move like a robot. Anyway, I had that particular teacher that day and he saw that I was a bit stiff. He asked me what was wrong and I told him. During class, I was talking to my mate when the teacher came up behind me and belted me on the back with a T-square, causing all of the blisters on my back to burst. My shirt and shorts were soaked with whatever that fluid is inside a blister. It was disgusting and it hurt like crap. That's the type of teacher he was. It wasn't just with me. It was with everyone. He really shouldn't have been a teacher. Having said that, he was very encouraging when you did good work, and I appreciated that.

At one stage, a friend of his was suspected of killing his own wife and putting her through a meat-mincing machine at his pet food business in Walgett. We had to go out in stinking forty-degree heat and troll through the decaying kangaroo and pig carcasses to search for human remains. She was never found. I was told in no uncertain terms by my patrol commander to watch who I associated with.

While I was in Walgett, I had to travel back to Sydney several times to attend court and I caught up with Jann every now and again. She snuck me into the nurses' quarters at the hospital where she worked at the time. We did what we always did when we caught up, which always played havoc with my emotions. On my way out early in the morning, I opened her door and the girl who was staying directly opposite her room came out at the same time – Jenny, from high school.

'Hi, Mitch. What are you doing here?' she asked.

I was in my police uniform at the time, so I said, 'Just interviewing a witness to a serious crime.'

Unfortunately, she didn't buy it. Maybe the fact that I couldn't keep a straight face had something to do with it.

After my liaison with Jann, I made my way back to Walgett. It's a long drive and I had plenty of time to think. Too much time. All I ever thought about was Jann and why she treated me as she did.

I really enjoyed being in Walgett for the first twelve months of my two-year tenure, but after Sergeant Barnett arrived, he made my life hell, and I hadn't even touched his bloody daughter. He had never forgotten when I'd embarrassed him at the academy. He was an officer-survivor instructor and I was a trainee. He was giving us instruction on how to control members of the public in a protest situation when they have their arms interlocked. In the demonstration, he asked me to get out of his hold. I did so quite easily and punched him in the balls. Not a good idea. Now I was paying for it. All the shit shifts, all the crap jobs. I only had twelve more months to wait until I could leave.

Work wasn't everything. I used to play squash, tennis, golf, rugby union, cricket, and table tennis. I even used to go hunting, which I enjoyed. Not just to kill feral pigs and foxes: I liked the alone time. It used to help me relax and it provided a good source of exercise. I used to walk five to ten kilometres on a hunt.

The station had received a report of a dog attacking sheep out on the Collarenabri Road. One nightshift, I decided to get in the truck and go and have a look. Lo and behold, I saw it. Big bugger jumping on this sheep and wrapping its jaws around the neck of the sheep.

I wound down the passenger window, grabbed my .22 caliber rifle, took aim, and fired. Bonk. I thought to myself, *That was a funny sound.* The dog ran off. I didn't know if I'd wounded it or missed it altogether. I had a look around for it but couldn't find it. It was just starting to get light so I headed back to the station. When I got back to the station, I started to pack up the truck and went to wind the passenger window up. It only went up halfway. On closer inspection, I realised what the funny noise had been. I had shot the truck. My bullet had struck the slide channel that the window slides up and down in to open and close it. Needless to say, the boss wasn't happy. The boss made me pay for it as well.

Another time, I was at the station on my own when a lady came in to report that a young calf had been hit by a truck on the Lightning Ridge Road. I locked the station and went for a drive. I saw this young calf on the side of the road; just the calf and its mum. Mum was standing, watching my every move, walking back and forth but not getting any closer. The calf was just standing there but not moving. It was dribbling heavily. It was obviously injured and in a lot of pain as it couldn't get out of the mud. I decided to do the only humane thing and that was to put it out of its misery. I stood in front of it, drew my revolver, aimed directly between the eyes, and fired. The calf dropped to its knees and then onto its side. It was dead.

Mum wasn't too pleased, as you can imagine, and I felt deeply for what she must be thinking. I said, 'Sorry girl, but I had no option.'

I got back into my police truck and returned to the station. As I was at the front desk filling out the paperwork, I saw a farmer pull up out the front of the police station. He came storming in and said, 'Some arsehole has just shot one of my calves out on the Ridge Road.'

I said, 'Yeah mate, that was me. I'm sorry.'

He said, 'What the fuck did you do that for?'

I said, 'A lady came into the station and told me that she had just seen it get hit by a truck and it was badly injured.'

'You bloody idiot! The calf that got hit by the truck is further up the road. That one was just tired from being stuck in the mud.'

OOPS!

'At least you'll have nice tender beef tonight.'

I shouldn't have said that. After I got my arse well and truly reamed by the boss, I had to go and apologise. The farmer was the captain of our rugby side. Now I understand why I was never picked to play in the grand final side that year.

* * * *

On Christmas Day, 1988, Sergeant Evens and I were recalled to duty to attend a riot at Goodooga, just south of the New South Wales – Queensland Border. I had ten minutes to get my shit together for an operation with no finish date confirmed. We jumped in the police LandCruiser and headed up. I didn't know how bad it was. All I knew was that it was Sergeant Evens and me, and only us. I had just been promoted to Constable First Class, so I was quite happy until we got to Goodooga. That soon changed.

Goodooga is like a town from the old west: one main street, a medical clinic/hospital, a police station, a hotel motel/post office, and tumbleweed rolling down the main street. Blink and you'd miss it. If they were going to give the world an enema, they'd stick it up Goodooga.

Our first port of call was the police station. The local policeman was on annual leave and couldn't be contacted, so we got set up and were ready to go. We then did a quick patrol of the town to gauge what the mood was prior to attending the hospital. We obtained statements from those from both sides of the conflict. We found out that the aggressors were from Brewarrina and had come up to cause trouble. Didn't these people know it was Christmas?

We also learned that retribution was being planned as we spoke. Sergeant Evens started talking tough, but I knew this wasn't a time for chest thumping. We got back into the truck and headed down to the main street. Sure enough, a large number of men from the local aboriginal community – probably thirty in number – were marching up the main street with bats, clubs, machetes, fence posts, iron bars; in fact, anything that could cause injury. It was reminiscent of a scene from the old Wild West.

Sergeant Evens pulled up in the middle of the road and the mob of angry men stopped for a minute. They were talking amongst themselves while looking at us. I decided to make the first move. I told Evens to wait there and keep the truck running, just in case a quick retreat was required. He had a frumpy-type physique and I was much fitter back then. I got out of the truck and started to walk towards them. I stopped halfway hoping they would send their leader to meet me.

Five of them started to walk towards me. I knew that, if they decided to rush me, I could take six of them out and Evens could take another six before we would be overcome and finished. That was assuming that we hit everyone we fired at. That'd be the day. I hoped that wasn't going to happen.

As they approached, I extended my hand to shake hands with the apparent leader. That way, I thought I could build an instant rapport with him. One man shook my hand. I said, 'My name's Mitch, what's yours?'

'Steven.'

I said, 'I hear you've had a bit of trouble up here, Steve. Can you tell me what happened?'

He replied, 'It's Steven.'

I apologised and he continued. 'Yeah man, those fuckin' Bree cunts come over 'ere and bashed the crap out of us for no reason. They smashed guitars; my brother got a broken arm and is in hospital. We're gunna kill them cunts.'

I said, 'We were just up at the hospital. What's your brother's name?'

'Eddy. Eddy Bungy.'

'Oh, yeah. I just spoke to Eddy. He seems like a good bloke. Why do you think all of this happened?' I asked.

He replied, 'Eddy's a top bloke. Don't worry about why it happened. You cunts aren't gunna do nuffin about it, so we're gunna fix um right up.'

I said, 'Do you know the people who did this?'

'Yeah. There's ...' and he started rattling off names.

I took out my official police notebook and started writing the names down. A hundred things were going through my mind at the time. I also thought that the longer I spoke calmly to these guys the less agitated they would be, lowering their adrenalin and testosterone levels. But Sergeant Evens, who was a bit of a hothead, had started heading down to where I was.

I had to think quickly. I said, 'Look Steve.'

'It's Steven!' he interjected.

I said, 'Sorry. Look, Steven, we're here to sort this out but, before we can do that, we need to get statements off everyone involved from your side so that we can take action against those idiots from Bree. What say you give us a chance to do our job and if you're not happy with that, then you can beat the shit out of them. There has to be a level of trust. If I can trust that you'll leave this to us, then I give you my word that this won't get swept under the carpet. What do ya say?'

'We're all fired up ready to go, Sarg!' he exclaimed.

I said, 'Look, Steven, I know very well you guys could bash the crap out of us, burn our truck, and then take on those dickheads from Bree. All that will achieve is that you'll spend a shitload of time in jail, when you should be sitting down and enjoying a nice Christmas lunch with your family. The other side of it is that you may get your arses kicked twice in the same day. What do you reckon?'

He said, 'I'll be back in a minute. Wait here.'

I couldn't believe he had the balls to tell me what to do. *I'll give you wait here*, I thought. He walked back to the group and they were talking for a while. Then they all turned and started walking back from where they'd come from.

Steven came back alone. 'Mitch, we'll take your advice and let ya do ya job. If nothing gets done, then we'll take matters into our own 'ands.'

I said, 'That's fair. Where is everyone so we can come and take statements?'

'I'll come with you and show ya the way,' Steven said.

We went to the aboriginal community and took statements and had a bit of a laugh. Steven's mum invited us to stay for lunch and at first I declined. However, when I saw the spread they had set up, I changed my mind pretty quickly I can tell you. For people who were poor and lived in oppressive conditions, they were very accommodating and the lunch was one of the most enjoyable I'd ever eaten. Roast pork, ham, baked potatoes and pumpkin, lots of different fruits. It was everything I liked and more. We were there for a couple of hours and then had to leave. We extended our gratitude to Mrs Bungy for her hospitality and to Steven for backing down. Sergeant Evens stayed relatively quiet during the whole thing, which was good, except for when he was asking his questions and wanting more pork.

We then left and did a further patrol of the town. It was clear that the protagonists had left town and that everything would be quiet from then on. We booked into the local motel for the night and I had a shower and a nap on my bed. It was hot: about forty-two degrees; but dry heat, so it was bearable. In Goodooga, as with most of those smaller isolated towns, the water comes from bores. The water itself is 'hard' which means the chemical make-up of the water is different from, say, Sydney water, or even water from Walgett. It feels slippery on the skin and soap won't lather up. It's a weird sensation, washing with it.

The next morning was Boxing Day. We were doing a patrol of the middle of town when Sergeant Evens spotted a couple of feral pigs in a vacant block. I was driving and he told me to stop the truck. I stopped and he jumped out, pulled out his revolver, and shot one of the pigs.

He was about to shoot the other one when a lady from the house next to the vacant block came running out yelling, 'AAAHHHHH! What are ya doin'? What are ya doin'?'

It was then that I saw a rope tied around the 'still-standing' pig's neck. I thought, *Yesterday I worked my guts out to gain a good rapport within this community, and one shot and his idiocy has taken us back to square one.*

As you'd expect, the lady was ranting and raving. Sergeant Evens was very apologetic. In an effort to calm the lady, Sergeant Evens offered to buy the pig and asked how much she wanted for it. She told him $50, and so Sergeant Evens handed over a $50 note and said she could also keep the pig. She was as happy as Larry and we were back in the good books again. She even asked us if we wanted to shoot the other pig for the same amount. We declined.

After lunch, we headed back to Walgett with no further problems anticipated. The file of the Goodooga incident was dispatched to the Brewarrina police who took over the investigation from their end. Numerous charges were laid and the penalties ranged from fines to terms of imprisonment. A good result.

As it turned out, 'we' were told by Sergeant Barnett that he would be recommending us for a bravery award. He never submitted the paperwork. If it had been anyone else, he would have. He loved to big-note himself in front of everyone. He was one of those blokes that 'needed' to be liked. A bit like me really. The only difference is that as a supervisor, he also needed respect, which he didn't get from anyone.

At least I know what I did that day, and nobody can take that away from me. I was very proud of what I had achieved on Christmas Day, 1988; although, in all honesty, I was shitting myself the whole time. I just didn't show it.

A copper named Jeff Austin had brought his Suzuki GSX1100R up to Walgett. He was showing it off behind the police station. I asked him if I could go for a ride. He said, 'Yeah, no problem but if you wreck it you pay for it.'

I jumped on the bike and took it for a ride up Lightning Ridge Road. I came to a long straight and gunned it. At 260 km/h, the sheep on the side of the road were just a blur. I pegged it back to a reasonable speed and then turned around to head back. I was approaching a bridge about three kilometres out of town. It was basically an 'S' bend. I slowed to forty on the approach and started the turn in. I didn't see the rock in front of me. It was about the size of a golf ball. I hit it with the front wheel which then skipped out, sending me and the bike into the side of the bridge.

I'll never forget the sound of crunching fiberglass, plastic, and metal. It was a deep grinding thud. I was thrown from the bike and onto the pavement on the bridge. It was an old timber bridge with wooden planks held down by big hexagonal exposed bolts then covered in bitumen. As I skidded on the bridge, I could feel the bolts tearing at my skin, opening up my flesh and leaving large areas skinless. I came to a stop and just lay there for a while, looking at the condition of the bike. In absolute agony, I tried to get up, but realised that my right foot was broken.

I hopped over to the bike and lifted it up, taking its entire weight on one foot. I swung my leg over the seat to get back on. The handlebars were at a very awkward angle. I tried to start the bike but it wouldn't start at first. After a few attempts, I could hear the battery starting to tire. I gave it one more attempt and, luckily, the bike came to life – albeit a sort of asthmatic, coughing and spluttering kind of life.

I rode the bike back through town and straight up to the hospital. I got off the bike and struggled to put the stand down. I thought, *I can't really damage it much more*, so I just dropped it. I hopped into the hospital and a nurse took one look at me and ran to help me. I was feeling faint and I collapsed just as she got to me. No waiting room for me. Straight in to see the doctor.

When I came to, I asked the doctor to phone the police station to let them know what happened. Shortly after, Jeff arrived. I didn't know what to say to him, so I just handed him the keys to the new Falcon I had just bought and told him to sell it.

He just laughed and said, 'Don't worry about it. Get fixed up and we'll work it out later.'

He was great about it. He eventually got the bike fixed and I did pay for it. I remained mates with Jeff until his transfer from Walgett. We never saw each other again.

* * * *

I decided to give Jann a call and we were chatting about this and that. She told me that she had met a guy, Ashley, who she quite liked. Although I tried to be a friend to her and listen to her news, I never liked hearing about her new men. In fact, I thought it was very insensitive of her to tell me about them. She must have known how it'd make me feel. I suppose that was a very unrealistic of me because I knew that at some stage she was going to find someone to love.

That night, I went out to the Sporto and got smashed. It wasn't a night I remember that well, which was the whole idea, I suppose. I actually wanted to forget a whole lot more. I had lost the woman I had fallen in love with and she had moved on. It was time for me to do the same.

Several weeks later, I was at a party in Newcastle. It was a friend of a friend's party, so I didn't really know too many people there. One girl caught my attention. Not really attractive, but fun. I went over and started talking to her. Janelle was her name – another country girl who loved to let loose. She was studying to be a teacher.

I gotta say, this girl gave me the best sex I have ever had. I had never had sex with a girl I had only just met, so I thought I'd feel a bit funny about it but, after that ... bring it on! I don't know if it was the amount of vodka she had consumed or if she just loved having sex but, I can honestly say, I didn't give a shit why she was that good. I instantly turned to religion and thanked God she chose me to do it with that night.

Janelle asked for my number, which I supplied without hesitation. But I also thought that, given her level of intoxication, she may not call. I headed back to Walgett the next day and still had a couple of days off, so I just rested. Little did I know that someone at the party had taken a happy snap of Janelle going to town on me and had it hastily developed and sent it back to the station.

The next night, I went to the RSL for dinner and drinks. Everyone knows everyone in Walgett, so there's always someone to talk to. At the time, there just happened to be a new batch of student teachers in town. As I was walking in, I saw a mutual friend of an old mate of mine. Suri was good friends with Rachelle and Leonard. I also would have been Suri's debutant partner if it weren't for that unfortunate motorbike accident.

Suri introduced me to Debbie, who was a very attractive lady. I thought to myself, *Wow, she's gorgeous!* She had the biggest eyes; stunning in fact, but, after you've been at Walgett for a while, a bent lamp post starts to look good. Debbie was talking to one of the boys so I let them be. I then turned around and saw this young lady really going to town trying to swallow Paul Monk, one of my footy team mates. She looked as though she knew what she was doing.

I turned to a bloke standing next to me and said, 'I'm going to marry that girl.' He laughed. I didn't. There was something about her that said to me, 'I'm yours'.

I said to Suri, 'Who's that?'

'Her name is Sophie. She's a prac teacher. Would you like an introduction?' she asked with a smile.

I just nodded.

Paul got up to go for a slash and I saw my opportunity. I grabbed Suri and pulled her by the shirt over to this beautiful girl now sitting alone, looking around the room as if she was lost. Sophie was about five foot four, a little over slight in build, with beautiful brown eyes and wavy brown hair. She was a typical girl-next-door type. She wasn't model material but she was very attractive. Suri introduced us and we sat and had a quick chat before Paul returned.

I went and had some dinner. I kept trying to see Sophie from my table but, suddenly, she disappeared. I finished dinner and went to look for her. She was sitting on her own again. I sat down again and she started to tell me all about herself, which was great, because I hate talking about me. I think the only thing I really heard was that she was going through a break-up and so she was single. I asked her if she wanted a drink but she refused. I got up to get one for myself and when I returned, she had gone. I thought to myself, *Rude bitch!* I then went home because I had an early shift in the morning. On the way home, I was thinking to myself, *I'm going to get to know her if it kills me.*

By the time I had started my next shift, the boys had pinned the naked photo of me and Janelle to the noticeboard in the meal room. When I walked in the whole place gave me a big cheer. I was about as embarrassed as anyone could get but, given the length of my dry spell, embarrassment soon turned to pride. Looking at the photo again, it was a great angle – probably my best side in fact.

Just prior to that shift finishing, I received a phone call. It was Janelle. I instantly thought, *Sensational!* She wanted me to come down again the next weekend but I was working. I told her I could make it the weekend after, and she seemed happy that I would be coming down to see her. I counted the days.

On the Friday, I finished at 3.00 pm. I was out the door and on my way by 3.30 pm. I must have made record time because I arrived at her house at 10.30 pm. We had a late dinner and sat and watched a bit of TV to wind down. She asked me if I was tired. I said I was stuffed.

'Oh,' she said, in a disappointed tone. 'Do you want me to wake you up?'

I smiled at her and said, 'That would be great.'

As we were walking to her bedroom, I saw a bloke in the hallway. 'G'day mate,' I said.

'G'day,' was the reply.

'Who's that?' I enquired. 'That's my flatmate's boyfriend,' she said.

'Good-o,' I replied.

There were no distractions and we had plenty of time on our hands. Janelle had lifted her standard even higher than before. I thought, *Is there a magic book about sex that this girl is reading?* That night was the 'new' best sex I had ever had. Who'd have thought the two best sexual experiences of my life were in succession with the same girl? Holy shit! And who ever thought that a girl would know how to do those things? It was ridiculous!

In the morning, I woke to breakfast in bed. Bacon and eggs. I thought to myself, *Jann never made me breakfast in bed.* Then I thought to myself, *Why the fuck am I still thinking about Jann?* That was the question to this irritating problem that kept hounding me but, to date, had remained unanswered. I only hoped that I would forget her sooner rather than later, before I went insane.

Just then, the door flung open. There, in the doorway, stood a tall redhead with a gorgeous body. I was shocked to see who was standing there and, clearly, so was she.

'Mitchell Walton!' she said in a disbelieving tone. 'How the hell are you? What are you doing here?'

It was Amanda – another girl from my Year 12 class from Chatham High School, in Taree. I began to wonder, *Are all my former classmates stalking me, or what?* I was still lying in bed naked after screwing her best friend all night.

We had a short awkward chat about this and that, before she gave me a cheeky little grin and said, 'Catchya,' and went back to her room.

I gotta say, she didn't look half bad herself. I got up and put my PJs back on and took the dishes out to the kitchen, when I saw the bloke I bumped into in the hall the night before. I looked at him, shook my head, and said, 'You lucky prick!'

He laughed. 'You sounded as if you did alright yourself.'

'No complaints here mate. See ya later,' I said, laughing.

I grabbed a towel and went to have a shower. I just jumped out of the shower when Amanda came in and started to clean her teeth. I was standing there, completely naked. No towel, nothing. I didn't know what to do, so I asked her what she was going to get up to that day, as I reached for my towel. We chatted for a bit as I started to dry myself off. She finished cleaning her teeth and said goodbye again, but not before having a little look up and down. There's something erotic about being checked out like that. At least she didn't laugh. That's always a good sign. Not that there's anything to laugh about.

Janelle and I went out to the Newcastle foreshore for the day. We had fish and chips for lunch, then went for a walk up to the lighthouse before heading back to her place around 4.00 pm. I told her about Amanda and the bathroom and she laughed. I packed my things and we said our goodbyes, as I had to get back to Walgett.

A few days later, I received a letter from Janelle. It read: 'Dear Mitch, Thanks for the wonderful time and especially the great sex. I want you to know that I care about you, but have decided to get back with my boyfriend. I hope you understand and don't hate me. Love, Janelle'. Short and sweet.

Why do I keep getting 'Dear Mitch' letters? I wondered. *Maybe I'm not that good in the cot ... Naaaaah. But who cares?* The funny thing was I wasn't upset. I was more upset that, after a great night of sex and brekky in bed, all I could think about was the fact that Jann never made me brekky in bed. Wow! This was becoming a habit. It was only then that I realised that I had another pattern thing going on with the girls I dated. Jann, Janette, Janelle. Now ... if I could only secure a 'Janine' a 'Janice' and a Jacinta, that would be cool!

In the meantime, I decided to give Jann a call to see how she was travelling. She told me that she was coming home for the holidays and suggested we catch up. I couldn't be happier but, also, couldn't be more pissed off. Here I was trying to forget her, romantically at least, and she wanted to catch up. I couldn't say no. She was like a magnet and I was steel. It was something nice to look forward to after all the stuff-ups at work. She told me she had to go to a function in Lightning Ridge, and then we could meet at the hot baths afterwards.

On the night, I drove up to the Ridge and waited at the baths. It was dark and she showed up in one of her dad's rickety old Toyotas. Every farmer had a rickety old 'something' to drive around in. I looked at her as she sat in the car looking at me through the window. She was the most beautiful girl I had ever seen. This was the girl I had been in love with since the day we'd met. I walked up to her, kissed her, and we started to chat: just about everyday things; life, friends, work, and so on. I asked if she wanted to go for a dip, but she refused, which surprised me. Jann never needed much of a reason for us to get our gear off together.

'It's too cold when you get out,' she replied.

I went in and it was beautiful. Hot and steamy. Just the way she liked it. She got out of the Toyota and I watched her walk towards me. She was wearing a gorgeous white dress. I couldn't believe that she was here to see me. She sat on the edge of the baths and we talked for an hour or so before I got out. It was freezing out of the water. She looked down and smiled.

She said, 'See, I told you it would be cold out.'

I looked down and she was right. Shrinkage is a bitch. My penis looked like a scared turtle trying to hide. I dried off and got dressed.

We had a little bit more of a chat in her car, before she told me that she had to go. Ashley, her new boyfriend, was in the back of my mind, but I leant across and kissed her. It was an amazing kiss. Not a long kiss, but very soft and sweet. I got out of the car and watched as she drove off into the darkness. I watched until I could no longer see her tail lights in the distance. The whole time I watched, I was hoping I would see her brake lights signal to me that she was stopping to come back. They didn't.

One week later, I received a letter from her. She told me how much she had enjoyed seeing me and that she would have done 'anything' that night. My heart sank and, at that moment, I realised that, on the night we met at the Ridge, I wasn't man enough to step up and take her as she had desired. Whether I misread her signals or just stuffed up, I knew that was my last opportunity and I had fucked it up. I had lost her forever.

Over the next few days, I was beside myself. I didn't know whether I was coming or going. I couldn't sit still. I was pacing. I was devastated. I did the only thing I could think of. I got pissed.

CHAPTER SEVEN

The next weekend, everyone was at the Sporto. I saw Sophie and Suri at the bar and Sophie was crying. I went over and sat beside her and asked her what was wrong. She explained that she had just found out that her boyfriend had been cheating on her. I sat with her and we talked. At closing time, we all went around to Kath Finlayson's place.

Kath's place was Walgett's party central. I don't think there was another venue. Anyway, I thought Sophie could do with some cheering up. After Kath kicked everyone out, we jumped in someone's car to get a lift home. Funnily enough, I only lived about 300 metres from Kath's house but, when Sophie got into the car, I got in the back seat with her. When we got to my place, I got out and looked at Sophie, leaned back in, and gave her a gentle kiss on the lips. She seemed receptive enough and I thought, *Cool!* As I got out of the car and turned around and looked at her, she smiled and gave me a little wave.

Over the next couple of weeks, we attended some barbeques and other events, but Sophie ended up going back to Armidale without giving me her phone number, so I called Suri to get it. For the next week, all I could think about was Sophie, so I called her. At the time, she was just getting ready to go to a fancy-dress party. She was dressed as a Christmas tree. In the brief time we did speak, we arranged for me to go and stay with her the next weekend. Maybe my luck had changed. I thought, *Ok, I'll call her again tomorrow.*

The next night came around and all was quiet in Walgett town. We had twenty-three police in Walgett with a population of 2,300 people. I must say, on that night, my 100 people were the best behaved in town. I saw this as my opportunity to call Sophie.

A girl picked up the phone. 'Rusden.'

I said, 'Is Sophie there please?'

'Hang on a minute,' she said. I heard her say, 'Sophie, I think it's him.'

I thought, *This could be a good thing or a bad thing.*
'Hello.'

'Hi, it's Mitchell,' I said.

'I was hoping it was you,' she replied, in a sweet flirty little voice. We chatted for only about ten minutes before she told me that she was on her way out, but she was looking forward to seeing me again.

It was a week of anticipation and nervousness. The boys at the station were egging me on to do some really 'sick' stuff and then give them all the details when I got back, but that's not my thing. It was with Janelle because she did some really 'sick' stuff. I mean 'sick' in a good way. But Sophie was different.

Friday week came around fairly slowly but, finally it arrived. I had to borrow a car from a mate from the courthouse because my car was a death trap. I had bought mine from one of the coppers at the station for $1,200 after I sold my car to pay for Austin's motorbike.

It was the first time I had seen Sophie in a few weeks. She looked sensational. She greeted me with a cheeky smile, and I gave her a kiss on the lips and a big hug. I love hugs. I couldn't believe how beautiful she was. Not only that ... she was interested in me. Wow!

I noticed her friends in the doorway of Rusden House looking on. I suppose they had to check out the new beau. I got the feeling they approved, but that wasn't important to me at the time. That evening, I thought we would go out to dinner together, but she had other ideas. She had organised a night out at their favourite drinking hole, 'The Newy'. It was a good night, as I saw a couple of other people I knew as well.

Greg Applegoose, my old sports master from Chatham High School in Taree, was there. I didn't have him as a class teacher, but I was heavily into sports. It's amazing how, sometimes, you really hate a teacher at school. However, after you leave and become a real working human being to them, all is forgotten. That wasn't the case on this occasion.

I said, 'Greg, how are you?'

He said, 'Ah, Mitch Walton. What have you been up to?'

I said, 'I joined the police force.'

'I didn't really think you'd amount to anything. Well done!'

'Greg,' I said, 'you were a fuckwit at school and you're still a fuckwit now. How do you stay so consistent?' Then I turned and walked away. To me, he was just an idiot. He may have been a teacher, but he never taught me anything. That says more about him than me, I think.

I looked around and saw Sophie looking over at me while she was chatting with her friends. Then I heard a voice from behind me. 'Hello, Mitch.' I turned around. It was a girl I knew from Taree. She used to go out with Paffy, my best mate. After she and Paffy broke up, we started to see each other, but I knew it wouldn't go anywhere because of the dreaded 'Bro Code'. It was a shame I had ethics because she was a 'really good sort'. I had a short chat with Linda but kept an eye on Sophie. When I saw a break in the conversation, I went over to Sophie so I could spend time with the girl I was there to be with.

I went and bought Sophie a top-up drink on the way over, and we grabbed a chair and sat for a while. At about 12.30 am, she asked if I wanted to go. We went back to Rusden and straight to her room. She had her own ensuite, as she was the senior resident. She was in there getting changed and doing, well, whatever it is that girls do in there, so I got into my PJs and slipped into bed. She turned the light off in the room, but left the light on in the bathroom. As she walked towards the bed, she looked at me and lent over and kissed me. She slid into bed and we had the most wonderful night together. I was very happy indeed.

The next morning, I had the unenviable task of walking into the kitchen with her. I had anticipated seeing others in the common kitchen, but not a dozen of them all smiling at me when I entered the room. It was one of those occasions when you don't know whether to smile and confirm their suspicions, or keep a straight face and keep them guessing. I decided to keep a straight face.

That day, Sophie had organised for us to go to this mystical destination called 'The Blue Hole'. It was supposed to be a place where there was a pond of unspeakable beauty. One day, I might like to go there. We got lost. It was quite funny because, here was this beautiful young lady who was, for some reason, attracted to me and trying to impress me. Regardless of her efforts, I was already impressed.

She was getting quite flustered, as she was trying to remember where this place was, so we decided to take a drive off the beaten track until we found another place. Not as beautiful as The Blue Hole might have been, but who cared. I was with a beautiful girl who wanted to be with me. Nothing else mattered.

After we had our lunch, we sat and had a chat and a kiss. I took a really good selfie, even if I do say so myself. I still have it in pride of place in the photo album. It was a really nice afternoon, but it was time to go. I had to make my way back to Walgett again for my next shift. It's fair to say that, when I left Sophie that afternoon, I had confirmed in my own mind what I had jokingly said to a mate in the club many weeks before – that I would marry this girl.

When I got back to Walgett, I gave Sophie a call to let her know I was home safely. We were on the phone for about an hour. We were already planning my next trip over to Armidale. Little did I know that she was also planning a surprise trip over to see me.

Two weeks and many phone calls had passed between us, when I received a message saying that I needed to contact Sophie urgently. I rang her straightaway, and she told me not to come because she had decided to go away with a group of friends from university. I felt quite dejected but accepted her apology. Because of my insecurity issues, I was wondering if she had met someone else and this was the beginning of the end. I was on arvo shift, and couldn't wait for it to be over so I could go home and sulk, which I did. To make matters worse, taking a piss was becoming increasingly painful.

I made an appointment with the doctor. 'Drop ya duds,' he instructed. He had a bit of a fiddle and bit of a squeeze. 'Have you been sleeping around?' he asked, in a matter-of-fact way.

I said, 'I've had two partners in the last month. That's it.' He said, 'Oh well, my son, one of them has given you a dose and that means you may have passed it on.'

'How do I know which one?' I asked.

'You don't. You'll have to tell both of them to go and get checked. As for you, it's penicillin.' He wrote me a prescription and I left. I was a very unhappy soul.

I didn't care about telling Janelle, so I didn't. If she gave it to me, she could find out herself. Sophie, on the other hand – that was a different story. How do you tell someone you have just met that you have an STD and that she needs to get herself checked?

I thought honesty was the best policy on this occasion, and so I just phoned her and told her. She seemed ok about it on the phone; however, I was hoping like mad that she really was. I didn't want to lose her before it really began.

The next day, I went shooting in the morning. The pickings were slim for that time of year. Not a pig in sight, but I got plenty of exercise trying. I then went to work for my 3.00–11.00 pm shift.

After nightfall, into the station walked Suri. She said, 'I've got a surprise for you', then in walked Sophie.

I couldn't believe she was there. I was smiling that much it was hurting my face. I didn't even know she was coming over. I trotted around the counter and gave her a big hug. It was at that stage that I realised she was quite tipsy.

Sergeant Western was slightly amused at her condition.

'We've been to the Sporto and had a couple of drinks,' she said.

'A couple?' I said.

She just laughed. I told her that I would see her after work. It was a very nice surprise to see her, instead of worrying if she was going to have it off with someone else or, worse still, not want anything to do with me because of the VD thing.

I told Sergeant Western that Sophie was the girl I was going to marry. He kindly proffered his odds at the marriage succeeding. He said we wouldn't last eighteen months. Sergeant Western didn't mean any malice in his prediction. He'd bet on two flies on a wall to see which one would fly away first. A funny man and a true gentleman, you knew exactly where you stood with Robert, which is exactly the way I liked it.

Sergeant Barnett and Sergeant Johanson? Both the biggest pains in the arse you could ever work with. Sergeant Barnett would try to be your mate one minute and, a minute later, he'd be kicking your arse and threatening you with the sack over the most minor infraction. At the same time, he'd condone the same action by another colleague, who happened to be the flavour of the month. I hated him. Maybe it was just me because I made him look like a dick down at the Police Academy.

Sergeant Johanson was just a lazy prick. We'd be flat out on a pension night at the zoo, running around like blue-arsed flies, and Sergeant Johanson would walk in and say, 'Mitch, old son, I'm just going down to check the river level. You're in charge', which meant, 'I'm a lazy prick and don't want to do any work. You guys sort it out'. It was always interesting working at Walgett.

CHAPTER EIGHT

A week later, I went over to Armidale to see Sophie. It was still very exciting to see her, as I was quickly falling in love. I arrived late on the Friday evening, so when I got there we just went to bed.

On Saturday morning, we had breakfast and then went and had a game of tennis. Being a very competitive man, I found it very difficult to lose gracefully without letting her know I was permitting her to win. Needless to say, it was quite funny listening to her gloat about her success on the court. She still maintains to this day that she beat me fair and square.

That night, we went out to dinner again and went for a drive up to the lookout. The lights of Armidale were particularly alluring and the setting was right. It was a cold night. We were standing in the car park. I took her in my arms and I kissed her as softly, yet passionately, as I could. I actually felt her body tremble. I still wonder to this day if she was rocked by my tenderness or if she was just cold. We kissed for a few moments and then drew apart. I looked deeply into her eyes and, without any warning to either of us, the words just came out.

'Marry me?' I asked.

She looked at me in bewilderment. Then, after a short pause, she smiled and asked, 'Really?'

I nodded and she said, 'Can I think about it for a while?'

I felt like a proper dick. I thought I'd blown it with the first woman who was really into me. I told her that it was alright to think about it. We went for another drive and then returned to Rusden to go to bed. I didn't sleep a wink. All night, I just stared at the ceiling wondering when Sophie was going to say something and what she was going to say.

On Sunday morning, we slept in a while. After brekky, we were lying on the floor of the common room watching a bit of TV and she looked at me every now and again and smiled. Not an awkward smile: a nice 'I love you' smile. I got a good vibe.

Dianne and Mariah came in and joined us. Mariah picked up that something was going on but didn't say anything right away. After a while, they got up and left and Sophie looked at me and simply said, 'Yes.'

This time it was me who threw out the question. 'Really?'

Again she said, 'Yes, but I don't want to tell anyone yet.'

I agreed. She wrapped her arms around me and gave me a big kiss. It was evident, from then on, that something had happened because Sophie had a smile on her face all the time. So did I. I could have had a pit bull chewing my left leg off and I would still have been smiling. I could not believe it ... I was engaged. We'd only been going out for one month.

In the afternoon, I had to return to Walgett. The trip took on a whole different dimension because of the anticipation I felt, as I wanted to get back and tell the guys I was engaged. Gavin Dunkley, a quiet yet very funny man, was very excited for me, which was really nice. He was one of the nicest blokes you could ever meet and a bloody good policeman. Even though he was junior to me, I took a lot of advice from him when it came to policing matters. We used to spar out the back of the station in a makeshift gym he'd concocted; that is, until I realised that he could punch really hard. Even with headgear on, he could rattle my cage. Sergeant Western was happy for me and so was Geoff, but everyone else seemed a little nonplussed, which was a bit disappointing.

We had decided that I had better meet Sophie's parents before we told them we were engaged, and the same with my mum and dad, so we had to keep it to ourselves until I could arrange annual leave to do the rounds.

Sophie had been home at her parent's place for a while after graduating from university. As I was always having a go at her for being in civilization and for me living in the dry, dusty outback, she decided to do something 'nice' for me. She told me to expect something in the mail, so I waited and waited for it to arrive. When it finally did, I had to go to the post office to pick it up because the manager there wasn't happy with it. He handed me this box the size of a shoe box. We looked at each other and I thought, *What the ...* I could tell he was thinking the same thing.

It was all gooey and sticky and smelt like vinegar. I took the parcel from him, apologised and took it outside. I wasn't game to take it home so I opened it on the footpath. Rotten, putrid bananas. They were that cooked they were almost liquid. My little apple dumpling had kindly decided to send me some bananas through the post in summer. What a little gem she was. I couldn't read the note because everything had turned to mush. I rang her and told her what I'd received and she nearly cried. It was so sweet.

CHAPTER NINE

Eventually, I secured annual leave and we decided to go and introduce ourselves to each-others parents and then announce our engagement and, finally, take a trip to the snow. I was going on a trip with my new fiancé.

Our first port of call was for me to meet Sophie's parents. Since Sophie had gone home after university, we arranged for me to meet her there.

I drove up the long dirt driveway to her parent's place in Dunbible, a small farming community near Murwillumbah on the New South Wales North Coast. Her parents, George and Marg, lived on a banana farm, which was on the side of a mountain. *More akin to mountain goats than anything else,* I thought.

I drove up to the house and Sophie opened the front door and greeted me with a big smile. She came out followed by her mum – a typical down-to-earth farmer's wife. I immediately drew a comparison to Judy, Jann's mum.

George was down in the shed doing whatever it was that he did down there. Marg offered me a cuppa which, after the long drive, I gladly accepted. After our cuppa and chat, we walked down to the shed and I met George for the first time.

I was fairly nervous and apprehensive, but I needn't have been. He was a softly spoken man of few words. He greeted me with a very soft handshake and a 'Hello, how are you?'

I said, 'I'm fine. Would you like a hand with anything?'

He gave a little chuckle. 'No, we'll be right. You go back up to the house and I'll be up when we're done here.' It was as if he thought that a copper wouldn't have it in him to do a decent day's work. So I proved him right and went back up to the house with Sophie and had a lay down, as I was stuffed from the nine-hour drive.

Sophie and I had already discussed how I would ask George for permission to marry her. After dinner, George started to do the washing up. Sophie gave me the nod to go and help, so I went into the kitchen, picked up the tea towel, and tried a bit of small talk first to ease into it. George was a very quiet man, so small talk didn't really work. It took me a little while, and we were about halfway through the dishes, when I just came out with it.

'I know Sophie and I haven't been going out that long, but I really love her, and I was wondering if it would be ok with you if I marry her,' I said.

George gave a little smirk and said, 'No ... but I don't suppose I could stop it anyway so you might as well go ahead. She's not pregnant is she?'

I didn't know how to reply. Firstly, there was the rejection, although I did realise he was joking. Secondly, I didn't know if he wanted us to wait a bit. Then, there was the 'pregnant' thing. I just said, 'Not that I know of.'

By this time, I was looking for somewhere to hide when I noticed Sophie and her mum peeking around the corner with big grins on their faces. I finished drying the dishes and then went into the lounge room to field all of the questions they wanted to ask about the man who was going to steal their youngest daughter from them. Little did I know at the time, that I had actually won a bet for Sophie with her dad. Two of her three sisters had shotgun weddings. George had bet her a thousand dollars she wouldn't get married without being pregnant first. I know we weren't married yet, but I was determined to get that thousand dollars for my bride, so we didn't do 'it' until we got married. Yeah, right! I used to call her my little fire cracker because, while she was small in stature, in the cot, boy, did she go off!

After a couple of days, it was time to hit the road and head south to Taree for Sophie to meet my parents. I was quite relaxed about the whole thing, because Sophie is a beautiful looking girl and I knew that Dad would be impressed. Mum would be more impressed that she was beautiful on the inside as well. Win-win for me. Sophie wasn't as nervous with my parents as I was with hers and she opened up straightaway. Mum and Dad loved her.

Dad took me downstairs and said to me, 'What's your secret? How did you manage that?'

I just laughed and said, 'The Walton charm, Dad. The Walton charm.'

We went back upstairs and had dinner, and then sat down and watched some TV. Mum and Dad had made up separate bedrooms for us, as had George and Marg. Bloody old people. So we fooled around a bit on the lounge after Mum and Dad went to bed, and then went to bed ourselves.

In the morning, we all got up to have breakfast and Dad, being his usual self, cooked breakfast for everyone. After breakfast, I said to Mum and Dad, 'We have something else we need to tell you.'

Mum said, 'What?'

'We're engaged,' I said, fairly dryly.

Mum nearly screamed the house down and Dad just laughed with excitement. There were hugs and kisses all round. I told them we were on our way to Sydney to get the ring made. It was two different reactions from two different families, but everyone was happy for us.

'When?' Mum demanded.

'About eighteen months or so.'

'Why so long?' she asked impatiently.

I explained, 'Because, I want to turn twenty-five first and it'll give us time to save and do other things.'

That was good enough for Dad, and he gave me a nod of approval to suggest that I had my head screwed on the right way.

The next day, we travelled to Sydney and had the rings designed and made. After that task was completed, we drove down to Jindabyne for a short break. It was absolutely beautiful at that time of year. There was snow only on the peaks of the mountains and the weather was stunning. The sun was shining and I decided that I would take Sophie out in a boat on the lake. We hired a boat and navigated our way up the lake. It was very cool even though it was midday. Sophie was taking plenty of snaps with the camera because the scenery was so stunning. I had this impulsive streak that made me do things without thinking, so I told Sophie to close her eyes because I had a surprise for her. I stripped down butt naked, stood up in the boat, and yelled at the top of my voice, 'I'm in Love.' I forgot about the camera.

She was laughing and went to take a photo. I tried to cover up so as not to shock any future viewers of the photo with my, well, let's just say, impressive credentials, and I nearly fell out of the boat. It was a great day and one that I would always remember. Good thing Sophie had already used up all of the film in the camera anyway.

CHAPTER TEN

Sophie had been offered a casual teaching position at Walgett Primary School, which was great, because now she had to move to Walgett and there would be no more long journeys travelling back and forth to Armidale.

At first, she moved in with me at the barracks. I did this without asking Stuart and Geoff and, although they didn't say anything right away, it became apparent that they weren't happy – Stuart in particular. In hindsight, I understood why but, at the time, she was cooking and cleaning and earning her keep, so to speak, so I couldn't see what the problem was. Apparently, the boys couldn't be boys with her in the house. She was only there two weeks and had to move out. I got the shits for a bit and took it out on the neighbour's rooster and dog.

Every morning after I finished nightshift, the bloody rooster from next door would crow its beak off. When the rooster started to crow, that set the dog off barking. I had the shits over couple of things so I hatched a plan. I'd shoot the bastard of a rooster and, hopefully, the dog would stop barking.

I grabbed my .22 rifle – the same one I'd shot the truck with. I lined up the rooster and pulled the trigger. It wasn't a clean shot and I didn't realise it at the time, but it was a masterstroke on my part. I went back into the house and watched an episode of *Days of our Lives*. This was Walgett, after all. We only had two television channels back then.

The rooster had obviously stopped crowing but it wasn't until a few days later, I noticed that the dog had stopped barking as well. Had my plan actually worked? What I didn't realise was that, when I shot the rooster and didn't kill it outright, it began flapping around in the dirt and the dog had come over to investigate. The neighbour had come out and thought the dog had attacked the rooster, so he took the dog out and shot it. As I said … masterstroke.

* * * *

Sophie moved in with Suri and Don. Don was the most beautiful person you could ever meet. Photos of him on his wall depicted a strong, strapping young man, standing tall in his Walgett Rugby League uniform. The reality was that, in his early twenties, Don had been the victim of a spear-tackle which left him in a wheelchair for the rest of his life; a full quadriplegic, unable to use any of his limbs. Through rehabilitation, he had learned to train his arm muscles to spasm to the point where he could operate an electric wheelchair and even write letters and feed himself, but not much more. He was reliant on an aid nurse daily for all of the functions that most people take for granted.

We used to sit him on the lounge and have a go with his electric wheelchair. I gotta say, the man was a master at using that thing. I never got the hang of it. He used to cringe every time I got in it. He knew that, either the furniture was going to be worse off, or the paint was coming off the wall. Either way, the ending wasn't going to be pretty.

Don used to take us to the good fishing holes as well. We'd set a trap and catch a yabby or two, stick them on a hook, and catch the best tasting freshwater fish in the world. Golden Perch or yellow belly. We'd take it home, wrap it in foil with lemon and butter and a few other things, and throw it in the slow combustion heater. Delicious!

Don could also drive a car. He had a Ford panel van which had been specially adapted for his condition. It was weird driving it because all of the functions were operated by the hands. He needed to be put in and taken out of the car but, other than that, he was a good driver. One day, he took me out shooting at his brother's farm. He saw a big pig so he was off. This wasn't an off-road car but he just tromped it.

We got to within twenty meters of this pig and Don hit the brakes. I jumped out and, by now, the pig was about 100 meters away, so I took aim and ... Bam! Pig goes down. I ran up to it and finished it off with a head shot. I then noticed a rustle in the grass. It was a little suckling pig about the size of a Chihuahua, but fatter. As I got closer it bolted. I chased after it but, every time I leant down to grab it, it'd change direction. So I ran, caught up, and kicked it up the bum. This sent it rolling on the ground and then I jumped on it. It was so cute. I picked it up and took it back to the car and put it in a box. We called it a day and drove home. This little pig must have been so scared because it never made a sound.

On our arrival home, I showed Sophie what I had caught. As I took it out of the box, I noticed that it was covered in lice. Sophie put some water in the laundry tub and we gave the little girl a bath to get rid of the lice. She came up looking quite decent for a wild pig. We decided to call her Sally ... Sally the sow.

We had also recently bought a border collie pup. We called him Ozwald D. Dog. Ozwald was the son of an Australian champion and was an amazing dog. Whenever we'd throw the ball to Pete, Don's dog, Ozwald wouldn't chase the ball, he'd try to round up Pete. We paid eighty dollars for him and were offered one thousand but we refused. He was a beautiful looking pup.

After only two days, Sally must have thought she was a dog and was playing with the others. I don't know how, but she found her way through the fence and got out. We didn't know where she was so we went for a walk. Ozwald also ran off up the road and around the corner. As we got up to the corner, there was Ozwald bringing Sally home. Absolutely amazing!

Ozwald was eventually killed by my brother – accidentally, of course. He threw a stick for Ozwald, who grabbed it the wrong way, and the stick punctured his tonsils. He hemorrhaged over two days until we found him dead in his kennel. The vet had been treating him for poisoning but still wanted me to pay the bill. No way that bill got paid. I was devastated; I should've take the thousand dollars when I had the chance.

I was later told by my patrol commander that it is illegal to keep wild pigs and that I had to get rid of Sally. It upset us because we had grown attached to her. The local aboriginal liaison officer put his hand up to take care of her, as it's not illegal for aboriginal people, only white fellas. Sally only lasted a couple of weeks. He looked after her alright. They ate her. Talk about breach of trust. I suppose I was just naïve.

* * * *

Don suggested that I move in to his house so that I could be with Sophie and I could also help him when he needed a hand, so I moved out of the barracks and moved in down the road. Stuart was happy because he now had the largest room with the ensuite.

In the meantime, every chance Sophie and I got, we'd jump in the car and go somewhere new. This was the el-cheapo car I bought off one of the coppers at the station – an old 1973 XB Falcon. It had holes in the floor so dirty roads weren't great, and there were plenty of dirt roads around there. Dust would just fill the cabin. It wasn't great but, after crashing Jeff's motorbike, it was all I could afford at the time, and it was mine.

The trouble with heading north, was that Jann's parent's place was only 100 kilometres up the road so, whenever we were up that way, I always thought of Jann, always wondered what she was up to. I knew, by this stage, that she was going out with Ashley, but didn't know the status of the relationship. I hadn't spoken to her for a while and was feeling like I was cheating on Sophie for wanting to.

One shift, when I was stationed at Collarenebri, I drove out to Paterson and saw Judy and David. I wasn't sure they'd remember me but they did. As I mentioned before ... salt of the earth people. They didn't mention Jann, so I didn't ask, even though I really wanted to know what she was doing. I just had a cuppa and a piece of cake and then left.

CHAPTER ELEVEN

It wasn't too much longer before my transfer came through. My new station was Lismore, about eighty kilometres south of the New South Wales – Queensland border, near the coast. Although I was glad to get out of Walgett, it was bittersweet because, in my mind, that was my last link to Jann.

It was a weird scenario being played out in my head. I was in love with two women at once, but only one of them loved me back and the other had probably forgotten I'd existed, but still had a tight hold on my heart. It was like Jann was a shadow that constantly followed me around in my head. I couldn't lose it no matter what I tried.

Sophie and I settled in a place called Goonellabah, just outside Lismore. We got married on 14 April 1990, the day after I turned twenty-five.

The night before our wedding, all of my family and closest friends got together and went out to the Murwillumbah RSL for the night. There was a band playing in the auditorium and we were having a great time. It was approaching midnight and Sophie had to leave, so I walked her outside to say goodbye until tomorrow. I tried to get back in, but the bouncer refused me entry, saying I was too drunk. I was just deliriously happy, I said. I hadn't had a drink all night. I was probably more sober than he was. He still wouldn't let me in. At that stage, my sister came out to see what was going on and, after further discussions, I was allowed to go back in and continue partying.

Our wedding day was the proudest day of my life up to that point. The week prior, it was raining cats and dogs and we thought it was going to be a miserable day. When I woke up in the morning, I looked out the window. There wasn't a cloud in the sky. I was feeling quite relaxed for most of the morning; however, as the time came to go to the church, it finally dawned on me that this was it.

Inside the chapel, the nerves began swelling within me. I couldn't sit still. I was pacing back and forth. My brother Max, best mate Brant, and cousin Ethan, were all there with me. For a short moment, my mind was with someone else and that shouldn't be the case. For about two minutes, I had doubts as to whether I was doing the right thing. Then it just hit me. It was at that point that I knew everything would be ok.

We walked into the church proper where all our family and friends were waiting. Everyone was looking at me and smiling. I tried to smile but the nerves were killing me. The ceremony started with the traditional wedding march. As I looked towards the back of the church, an angel appeared. Sophie looked absolutely stunning. As George escorted her towards me, my eyes started to well up with tears, but I controlled myself. She was the most beautiful girl I had ever seen. I already knew that, but it was then that I was positive that the girl I was supposed to be with was now standing beside me.

During the wedding rehearsals, we had decided to say our vows without any prompting from the minister. I went through my vows and needed a little prompting;

however, Sophie breezed through hers. Softly and lovingly she recited her vows. She was amazing!

The reception was held in a hall in Murwillumbah and everyone had a good time. The speeches were funny and the food was nice. It was a night I will never forget. Don made the trip from Walgett, which was appreciated. We hadn't seen him for a while. We hadn't seen a lot of family and friends for a while. It was great to catch up again.

When all the dancing and celebrations were nearing an end and it was time for us to go, everyone formed a circle and Sophie and I circled in opposite directions to thank everyone for coming. It was on more than one occasion that someone muttered to me, 'If you ever hurt her I'll kick your arse'. It is a moment I think about every time Jann enters my head.

We didn't tell anyone for obvious reasons but, because accommodation wasn't plentiful in Murwillumbah, we had arranged to stay at the same motel as everyone else. We went back to the motel, did what every newlywed couple does on their wedding night, and then went to sleep. We didn't sleep too well because all we heard all night were drunken 'rels' and friends making their way back to the motel. We were lying in bed trying to identify the voices as they came back. It was good fun.

When we got up in the morning, everyone looked at us and said, 'What are you doing here?'

I said, 'We stayed here last night.' They all got annoyed because they'd missed the chance to hassle us. I told them that's why we didn't say anything. That day, we travelled back down to Goonellabah, before heading off on our honeymoon.

For our honeymoon, we went to New Zealand – probably my favourite country at the time. We had ten days travelling the North Island in a campervan. I'd never used a campervan before. It was great fun. We made our way up to the Bay of Islands and took a cruise out to the 'Hole in the Rock'.

I don't know why I get on boats, as I always get seasick. The Captain asked everyone if they wanted to go through the 'Hole in the Rock'. Everyone obviously said 'yeah'. I was feeling a little bit squeamish by this time. Little did I know that on the other side was open ocean and heavy seas. Anyway, through we went. On the other side, I could feel myself starting to feel ill.

Sophie asked me if I was alright and, being the newly-married tough guy, I said, 'Yeah, I'm fine, why wouldn't I be?'

Then my worst nightmare came true. 'This is your captain speaking. Who wants to go through again?'

I grumbled, 'Noooo.' I mean, you've seen a hole in a rock once, why would you want to see it again? Has it changed that much in two minutes? By this time, I was as green as a lush country meadow and everyone could see it, but through we went again. I wish I had hurled but I didn't. I hung tough! When we landed at the dock, I couldn't get off fast enough. Solid ground had never felt so good.

One thing I did do on that honeymoon was have plenty of sex. Sometimes I even asked Sophie to join in! I had plenty of sex because I heard a God-awful rumour about the lack of sex after marriage, and I wasn't going to take any risks.

Soon after we got back from our honeymoon, we bought a block of land just around the corner in

Goonellabah. We then signed a contract with the builder to start as soon as possible. It was only a matter of weeks later that we decided to start a family. Well, I decided ... with a little help from Sophie I suppose. I hid her contraceptive pills and I think that gave her the hint.

I hadn't been aware of the difference between sex for sex's sake and sex for making babies. It wasn't until then that I realised the depth of my love for Sophie. I knew I loved her; but, wow – the moment a baby is made is truly enlightening! It was very sensual and emotional knowing that, at that moment in time, we were making another life to be brought into the world – our world. Little did we know that, upon her arrival on 5 February 1991, she would become our whole world. And I wouldn't have had it any other way.

Annie arrived at 4.15 am – the product of a night of alluring and passionate love (well, ten minutes of love – the rest of the night was spent cradling Sophie in my arms). When Annie arrived into the world I couldn't help but wonder how this all came about. She was the most chubby, beautiful baby I had ever seen. I loved her from the moment I saw her tiny scrunched-up face. She was perfect. When I held her for the first time, I knew I was in love all over again. You know how you look at some babies and you think, *Fuck, that's ugly! Someone forgot to close the cage at the zoo.* Well, Annie was a genuinely beautiful baby.

It was funny, because I had been waiting to do the water police course for ages and, just when Annie was due, my patrol commander told me the course was on and I had to be there. I missed the first two days of the course and I was really upset about it. I've always liked boats and had grown to love the water. I still get seasick – I can't help myself. As it turned out, I completed the course and I still topped the class despite missing a couple of days.

After spending time with Sophie and Annie, I had the task of informing the new grandparents. I didn't want to wake them at that hour, so I held off for a while. The person I did ring was Jann. I wanted to share the news of our new arrival with my 'distant shadow'. Needless to say, she wasn't impressed with the timing of the phone call and, in hindsight, I couldn't blame her. But at least I got to talk to her. What I was still trying to reconcile in my head was why I needed to. During that short conversation with Jann, She told me that she had married Ashley. I was glad she found happiness, but it hit me hard emotionally. I wasn't ready within myself for her to be with someone else.

A month after Annie graced us with her presence, our new house was finished. It was a modest three-bedroom house which I converted to a four-bedroom place myself. I loved that house. When we travel up north to see George and Marg, we'd always swing by and check it out. The gardens have matured but everything else has remained the same. The garage that Sophie's dad, brother-in-law, and I built still stands tall. I think it will be there long after the house is gone.

* * * *

On New Year's Eve 1991, I was rostered to work highway patrol in the Lismore – Ballina – Byron Bay area. It was a great area to work. At about 11.00 pm, I was at the corner of Rotary Drive and Ballina Road in Lismore when I noticed a vehicle travelling at excessive speed heading towards Ballina. I took off after it and followed it for about half a kilometre to observe the vehicle's speed: 104km/h in a 60 km/h zone.

I had my lights on high beam and the vehicle appeared to have only the driver on board. I activated the emergency beacons and flashed my headlights at the driver to pull over. As I did that, I saw a second person's head bob up into the passenger side of the car from a position which appeared to be from the vicinity of the driver's lap. They must have been having a nap. The car pulled over and I got out of the police car and approached. As I looked into the driver's window, I noticed that the driver's pants were down around his ankles.

I said, 'Can I see your licence please, Sir?'

The driver said, 'Can you give me a few moments to compose myself?'

I said, 'You can do that while I check the details of your licence.' He then handed me his licence.

I couldn't help noticing that the man was in a very excited state and so I just had to see what his partner in the passenger seat looked like. I returned to speak to the driver about his speeding and leant down to have a perv at the passenger, only to find an unattractive bearded man, also with his trousers undone.

I managed to restrain myself from blurting out something inappropriate, instead saying, 'Sir, I recorded your speed at 104 km/h in a 60 zone. Do you have an explanation as to why you were travelling at that speed, even though I can hazard a guess?' I couldn't help myself.

He said, 'I guess I was just a bit excited to get to Ballina for New Year's Eve.'

I said, 'I bet you were. I'm issuing you with a traffic infringement notice for exceeding the speed limit by more than 35 km/h. It carries with it a $500 fine. You have twenty-eight days to pay. If you fail to pay, you will be given a further twenty-eight days to pay before your licence is cancelled. Another 1 km/h, Sir, and I would have suspended your licence on the spot. Do you understand that?'

'Yes.'

I said, 'Keep it in your pants while you're driving and have a good evening.' I then headed directly to Byron Bay, because that's where the action was on New Year's.

I arrived in Byron shortly before midnight. I couldn't believe the number of people in the streets, in the bars and on the beach. The local police used to call Byron 'The Pet Shop' ... pussy everywhere, and a few dogs as well. It was funny how many girls seem to lose their inhibitions when they have had a few too many. The number of girls having sex on the beach in broad view of anybody walking by was amazing. Maybe it sounds as though I'm saying that it's ok for blokes, but not for girls. I'm not. It's just that usually, guys don't mind being busted. It's like a badge of honour. Girls are usually more modest about where they do it. Not on New Year's Eve though, and obviously not in Byron Bay. Because of the fights, car accidents, random breath testing activities and so on, we had to patrol the whole township throughout the night, so we didn't really have time to perv ... I mean lock them up for having sex in public. If we did try to lock them up they usually tried to make a move on us. Not always a bad thing, but not part of our normal duties.

It's phenomenal the number of times I've been propositioned by females to get out of a ticket. I didn't tell Sophie because I didn't want to worry her, but the offers came from all types: young P-platers, young mums, older women. I even had a proposition once from a bloke offering me his girlfriend, who was asleep in the back seat, because one more ticket would result in him losing his licence. I actually let him off with a warning, not because I took him up on his offer, but because I reckon if she found out what he'd offered, he wouldn't need his licence anymore because he'd be dead. For the record, I never did take anyone up on their offer, although it did make me feel good. I had not been married long and was very much in love with Sophie.

When I finished my rotation with the highway patrol, I seriously considered requesting a transfer to that section. I thought about it; however, I liked the variation that came with general duties policing. At the time, I also thought I had friends in the general duties section, but that was just a fallacy. I don't believe anyone is really friends with anyone else in the police force. You might get on with one another but that's it. To give an example: Sophie threw a party for me when I received my first stripe. Most of my work colleagues came along and even the guys on duty made a short appearance. Then, when I got assaulted at a later time and there was some suspicion surrounding the circumstances, nobody showed up to support me.

Sometimes, when we were bored at the station, we'd have a competition to see who could go out and write the most tickets in a shift, or who could write the most expensive ticket, or the most ridiculous. I actually have the honour of being the first policeman in New South Wales to write a ticket for someone talking on their mobile phone while driving. My most unusual ticket was for a bus driver for 'splashing water on a pedestrian by an omnibus'. But my most ridiculous ticket was given on a Saturday night. A guy and a girl were embraced in a passionate kiss in the back seat of a taxi, so I pulled the taxi over and gave them a ticket for not wearing their seatbelts. It just so happened that the guy was a friend of one of the cops I worked with. I wasn't too popular but I think I had all the major categories covered.

One of the coppers, Brian Pike, was so bored after an arvo shift one evening, he decided to go and chase rabbits on the football fields behind the offices of the Northern Star in Goonellabah. Unfortunately, it had been raining and he got bogged right in the middle of the field. When the next issue of the *Northern Star* came out, his car was centre stage on the front page. I thought it was hilarious but the boss didn't. Needless to say, there was a bit of serious arse-kissing by Brian to save his own backside over that.

Not long after that, a mate of mine, Scott, was transferred from Orange to Lismore because he'd been caught shoplifting. He was very embarrassed and didn't like to talk about it. Typical police department didn't want to deal with issues like that so they just shifted the problem to another station. The problem was that it wasn't a one-off. Six months after he arrived, he got caught stealing some spark plugs from Kmart. He did a 'bolt' and hid in a wheelie bin.

Word soon got around and one of the guys at work, who fancied himself a cartoonist, plastered a cartoon up every time Scott had a shift. Given that he was on restricted duties, he couldn't help but see them. A week after the cartoons went up, Scott went missing. Two days later, they found him at Chatsworth Island, near Grafton on the north coast of New South Wales, with a .303 rifle at his feet and his brains splattered over the ceiling of his car and half his head missing. And I did nothing to stop the ridicule. I was his mate … and I did nothing. That says volumes about my character, and his courage.

Scott made mistakes but we all do. People said Scott took the easy way out, but I know he didn't. To take a gun, place it under your chin, and pull the trigger, wondering if it will hurt but knowing that, in a nanosecond, you are about to be reduced to a piece of meat on a cutter's table at the morgue, leaving behind everyone you love and everyone who loves you – that's courage. I'm not saying it's not courageous to face your demons and stare them down but, in his mind, Scott did not have a choice. People with mental illness don't choose – they react. It was one of the few times I had to leave work early, go home, and be with Sophie.

My sister, Sasha, had joined the police force after me. She got the station I wanted – Kings Cross. It was great having another cop in the family. When we got together it was like we were in our own little world. Nobody else understands police like police. That is why, when you are a member of the police force, you are part of a family. When you leave, it's as if you never joined. They wipe you clean. Now I hate 'em all. They're arseholes, the lot of them. Sasha and I use to be as thick as thieves when we got together. We'd share stories, back and forth, that were both funny and sad. Police have an uncanny way though of making sad stories funny. It's just the way they are. The dark humour disguises their true feelings about the things they see; things that no one should ever have to see. So to be cast aside by people you considered friends once you leave is a bitter pill to swallow. Just because you leave, doesn't mean you instantly forget those things that give you nightmares. That's why when I get pulled over by a police officer for a traffic offence I get the shits. Not because they don't let me off, but because they don't show the respect that I think I deserve for going through what they go through and, in most cases, more.

CHAPTER TWELVE

One night, in July, 1992, I was rostered on nightshift from 11.00 pm to 7.30 am. This was the night that changed my life forever. As usual, I went to bed early in the evening. I heard the alarm and I got up quietly, as Sophie had not long come to bed and had already gone to sleep. I dressed in full police uniform, kissed Sophie goodnight, and headed out the back door.

There was an empty paddock at the rear of our house where I used to park the car on nightshift so I wouldn't wake Sophie and Annie when I left the house. On this particular night, as I walked out the back towards my car, I could smell a very strong scent of petrol. It smelt like it was coming from my car, so I approached and opened the passenger door, which was ajar. The interior of the car was soaked in petrol and the fumes were overpowering. The next thing I knew, I felt a big thud on the back of my head and the lights went out.

I came to sometime later in my backyard, as ambulance officers were shoving an IV drip into my hand. I could see a flicker of flames reflecting off the windows of my house. It wasn't until I was turned over and loaded onto a stretcher, that I saw my car completely engulfed in flames. There were police everywhere – the neighbours were in our yard, and Sophie was crying. I was taken to Lismore Base Hospital where I remained for three days with heavy concussion.

Following the assault and fire-bombing of my car and the incompetence of the detectives at Lismore Police who did not manage to catch the offender, I fell into a state of deep depression. I underwent various levels of psychological treatment, including medication and 'on the couch' therapy. This took place over many months. I took extended periods of time off work and these eventually led to a transfer to Hornsby Police Station in mid-1993.

I was not only suffering from the effects of the assault in Lismore, I also began to experience the long-term effects of being bullied when I was a child. All of my demons were attacking me at once and in large numbers. Unfortunately, by the time I was in my mid-twenties, I had become an expert at hiding the symptoms ... until that point.

In the meantime, Sophie had fallen pregnant again with our second baby. This added another dimension to my already sky-high stress and anxiety levels. Sophie was not coping well with my depression and I was worried that this would have an effect on her and our baby. Sophie is a woman who hides her emotions well ... to a point. She is the most supportive influence in my life and I don't think I would be here today if it wasn't for her.

At the time Sophie was due, I was supposed to start at Hornsby Police Station. I had been down to Sydney previously to find a house to rent, but couldn't find one in an area that I liked. On the way back, I had a look at the Central Coast and really liked it. I signed a lease on a three-bedroom house in Kariong. So, I went back up to Goonellabah to start packing. I knew it would be touch and go as to whether Sophie would make the distance before giving birth and, as it turned out, she didn't. Taree was as far as we got.

We located an obstetrician in a hurry and she was admitted to Manning District Hospital where baby number two, Siion, was born on 22 April 1993. This time it was at a more respectable hour – around 3.15 pm. Siion was also a beautiful-looking baby. It was a funny thought, but I looked at her wondering if all the stress that Sophie and I were undergoing would be passed onto her.

As it turned out, it was actually a good thing having Siion in Taree as my mum and dad lived nearby. While Sophie and Siion were resting at Mum and Dad's place, Dad and I went down to the house I had rented and met the removalist truck to unload all of our stuff. Dad said, 'You know Sophie's not going to like this, don't you?' I told him she'd be alright.

We went back up to Taree for another couple of days, then all four of us made the final journey to Kariong. Dad was right. Sophie didn't like it. No storage in the house at all. I had all the storage I needed in the garage. What possible storage do you need in a house? Pantry … no. Linen cupboard … no. Adequate kitchen storage … no. Down town to buy some storage cupboards. Problem fixed.

The other problem was much harder to fix though. The separation anxiety Sophie felt was substantial. She tried to hide the tears but I knew she was suffering. I told her that she could phone her family as often and for as long as she needed. It didn't completely fix the problem but it did help.

Sophie found her feet reasonably quickly on the Central Coast. She joined a playgroup and made friends very easily. She's a very likable person. Who wouldn't want to be friends with her? I'm much more guarded with whom I let in. She also got the word out to the different schools on the coast and quickly became a sought-after casual teacher. She was never out of work; except when she wanted to be. Those two things kept Sophie's thoughts occupied while I wasn't around but, when I walked through the door at night, I could always tell she was worried about me. It's not a nice feeling to know that you can't provide your wife with a sense of wellbeing. That is one dimension of our marriage where I feel that I have failed her. I am supposed to protect her, and I didn't.

* * * *

Although the move to the Central Coast and a new baby was a fresh start, it wasn't the silver bullet that would fix our problems … my problems. My very first shift at Hornsby Police Station was one of despair, and would be one that would set the tone for the next twelve months of my life, as well as spell the beginning of the end of my police career.

During the shift, I had been given a tour of the patrol area and dealt with a young female teenage drowning victim who had been removed from life-support. She had drowned at a school swimming carnival. How tragic is that? I was also accused by a senior officer of not wearing my hat while out of the car at a serious motor vehicle accident, at which time a four-year old girl had been unrestrained, thrown from the vehicle and, subsequently, died in my arms at the scene.

In my eight years of service, I had seen many fatalities as a result of car accidents, but none had as much impact on me as that little girl who, through no fault of her own, lost her life that day. Her name was Sarah and I was devastated for her and the family she left behind. I never spoke of this to Sophie, although, maybe I should have. I didn't want to burden her with what went on at work, but bottling that up wasn't healthy.

I tore Inspector Burton a new arsehole after he reprimanded me for not wearing my hat under such circumstances. He claimed he didn't know about Sarah. A heated discussion took place and it was decided that we had best keep out of each other's way. He was a prick and that was one fucked-up day.

The one thing I did earn out of the confrontation with Burton was the respect of most of the sergeants at the station. Word had quickly spread about what had happened and that I wouldn't take any shit … from anyone. As a result, I was treated no differently to the many other police stationed at Hornsby, which is how I wanted it to be.

One sergeant in particular, Bruce Steel, knew Jann's dad, David. In fact, he used to play football with him out west. He shared quite a few stories regarding David that made me laugh and think, *So that's where Jann got that from*. Having said that, Jann was far more like her mum, Judy. Jann was very close to her mum and it was evident when they were together.

It was the first time in quite a while that I had thought about Jann. However, one thing I did realise was that I missed her. The moment I started to think about her again, my stomach started to churn and twist. I tried to do a computer search to find her but Sergeant Steel kicked my arse. It was against police regulations to use the computer for personal purposes, and I knew it. Sergeant Steel told me that if it were anybody else, they'd be out of a job. I appreciated him looking out for me as I think that, during our conversations, he'd realised what Jann meant to me. He told me to pull my head in and reminded me that I was married and to get over Jann: advice I could have reminded him of when it came to female clients.

I later learned that, at that time, Jann and I were closer than we had realised. She was nursing at Hornsby Hospital and I was at Hornsby Police Station. That could have been a very interesting episode in both our lives, had we known about it at the time.

* * * *

I started to think about Jann a lot; I began to have all sorts of erotic thoughts about her. I had finished an afternoon shift one night and was absolutely stuffed. I was on the train on my way home from Sydney late that night. The train pulled into Hornsby and the last person got off. I got on and went downstairs. I was alone. Just as the doors started to close, I saw a woman jump on at the last minute. I couldn't see her face as she was obstructed by the vestibule wall of the train; however, I heard her speaking on her phone.

I was amazed at how familiar her voice sounded. I listened a little longer and couldn't help but notice the little nuances in her voice that made it sound so familiar. I couldn't resist the temptation to have a look, so I got up and moved towards her. She was facing the other way, so I had to walk past her and glance back. As I turned to her, she looked up. Our eyes met. It was her.

We looked at each other for a moment. She said to the person on the other end of the phone, 'I'll call you back,' and hung up.

I walked back to her without saying a word and kissed her like I've never kissed anyone before. She didn't resist.

The passion was intense, yet there was tenderness. The feel of her body against mine was pure heaven. Our lips parted and we gazed into each other's eyes.

She took me by the hand and led me to the triple seat at the end of the carriage. Our eyes never wandered as we undressed each other. It was the most sensual feeling I have ever had. I couldn't take my eyes off her. I picked her up and gently laid her down. I paused for a moment to take in her beauty. As I lay on top of her, I kissed her again, firstly on the lips, then the ears, then the neck, at the same time running my fingers through her hair with one hand and gently stroking her thigh with the other.

I started moving slowly south. I didn't neglect one part of her body; her shoulders, her hands, her breasts. The warmth I felt was as beautiful and sensual as I'd remembered from so long ago. I could feel her body trembling uncontrollably with pleasure. I was feeling so aroused that my moisture-seeking missile felt ready to launch early, so I kept her hands well clear of the danger zone. I kissed her tummy and then her thighs, while holding her gently by the hips. I could feel her body heaving with the anticipation of what was to come. She wanted me inside her. I knew it. She took my hand and placed it on her warm wet pussy, forcing my fingers inside her.

I started caressing her pussy, parting her lips and then penetrating her with my tongue, sliding my fingers in and out of her love tunnel, causing a cascade of love juice to flow down her inner thighs. The taste of her drove me crazy. I found her sweet spot with my tongue. She was convulsing with pleasure as I slid my tongue over her clitoris.

It didn't take long. The sweet feminine moans of pleasure gave way to a crescendo of soft screams asking me to keep going; demanding me to keep going. Suddenly, a rush of moisture filled my mouth as her body stiffened prior to the release of tension as she reached orgasm. I felt her body tremble. I looked up and saw her face. A sense of calmness came over her.

As she relaxed, my passion rose exponentially. She was so wet when I entered her that I slid in and out with ease. I could feel my long hard cock pressing against the furthest reaches of her inner woman. The rocking of the train accentuated my pulsating penis; the 'clickety-clack, clickety-clack' of the train on the tracks providing the perfect metronome-like rhythm with which to thrust deep into her; thrust slowly, deeply, but oh so tenderly, while looking directly into her eyes, deep into her soul.

She wrapped her legs around me pulling me deeper again. She then rolled me onto my back. I lifted my arse off the seat and pushed hard into her. As she rocked on top of me, I could see the rapture building on her face once again. I stroked her breasts; I could feel the ecstasy pounding out from her thumping heart as she came once more, soaking me and the seat with her love syrup. She kissed me passionately as she lifted herself off my still hard love pump. As she started to go down, she was looking at me with a cheeky, yet seductive, grin as if to say, get ready. And she didn't disappoint.

I watched as my cock, still glistening with her cum, disappeared into her mouth. Her motion was seamless and sensual. Twirling her tongue around the head, then up and down my shaft and deep into her mouth again. She squeezed her lips together tighter and slid my member in and out, faster and faster, until I couldn't hold it any longer. I began to release and I unloaded with such ferocity that it almost hurt. She knew the exact moment I exploded, and withdrew just in time to watch the eruption of semen gush from my rock-hard penis. My cum squirted over her lips, cascading down her chin onto her breasts. She gathered up my cum and slowly caressed it over her love button.

She continued to slide her hand up and down my shaft of pleasure for a short time, while never breaking her heart-piercing gaze into my eyes and deep into my soul. As she made her way up my body, I could feel both our hearts beating as one and I felt totally at home with the woman I loved. We kissed again and I could taste the slight sourness of my cum on her lips. My desire for her was uncontrollable.

We lay for a short while in each other's arms. As the train approached my stop, I was looking for a signal that she wanted me to stay, but I knew our lives were different and she knew that as well. As I left the train, I turned and smiled and she smiled back and whispered, 'I love you'. Words that I had longed to hear. The vision of her smile will be burned into my soul for all eternity. I left the train and watched with despair as the red tail lights of the train disappeared into the distance, wondering if, one day, we would be as one.

Suddenly, I felt a hand on my shoulder, shaking me. 'Mate, it's time to get off. The train has terminated.'

I looked up and I was at Wyong. I had meant to get off at Gosford. It felt so real I had to check where I was seated. I even had a look at the seat at the end of the carriage as I left, just to make sure. Damn!

I will never forget that precious time spent with my Jann on the train, even though it was only a dream. In reality, I don't even know if she's still alive. All I know is that she has an emotional stranglehold over me that I fear can never be broken … ever.

The next day, I tried to find Jann through the telephone directory network. I had exhausted every piece of information I knew about her and her husband; where they had lived, where I thought they may be. I was at a loss. I didn't know what to do so I tried to forget … again.

Time marched on and, although my feelings for Jann were still there, they were suppressed by the memories I was making with Sophie and my two darling girls.

* * * *

My ten-year reunion for Year 12 had been arranged and I couldn't wait to go. I was very nervous, but excited to see everyone. As was to be expected, not everyone showed up, but those who did had a great time. Any petty differences people had felt at school were long forgotten. Two of the blokes I used to hang out with came up to me, which was great until the time came to introduce them to my wife; which is exactly how I introduced her … as my wife. I had developed a nervous mental block and had forgotten her name. Luckily, she saved me from total humiliation and chimed in and introduced herself.

The next day, we had a recovery day at Saltwater Beach. This was mostly for the kids; however, it was really nice to catch up with everyone. As usual, everyone promised to keep in contact, but didn't. Maybe it's just me. Maybe it's just that people prefer to remember the past fondly, but look to the future. I'm not like that. I like the past. I'm sure that if they had an Eighties museum, I'd be stuck in it. I really do miss that time of my life. I'm not a 'future' kind of guy. To me it means uncertainty, and I like to know what's going on. I know what went on in the past and I'm happy with that – except for the bullying. I'm probably a bit of a weirdo, I think.

CHAPTER THIRTEEN

I was still suffering from severe anxiety and stress as a result of what happened in Lismore and the upheaval we endured during the move to the Central Coast. Despite this, Sophie and I decided to buy a block of land in Kariong and build a house.

In 1994, we moved into our new house at Kariong. It was so much better than the dump we had been renting. I installed parquetry flooring throughout the whole house and it was magnificent, even if I do say so myself. One thing I've always prided myself on is meticulous attention to detail.

I was rostered on to assist the station officer at Hornsby. At the time, the firearm amnesty was in effect and people were handing in all sorts of unused and unwanted firearms for disposal. The firearms amnesty allowed members of the public to dispose of unregistered and illegal firearms and other prohibited weapons, without penalty, if handed into a police station within a specific timeframe.

During the course of the shift, a police officer asked me to keep an eye out for a particular type of rifle he was after for his collection. Although the practice was illegal and ostensibly frowned upon by the establishment, it was generally accepted within the rank and file that, if there was a firearm that looked too good to hit the furnace, it wouldn't go into the 'surrendered firearms' book or the exhibit/property room.

It was an amazing coincidence that, during that shift, a lady did hand in a firearm similar to the one requested by the police officer. I didn't realise at the time that I had been set up. I never was 'the sharpest tool in the shed'. I'd finished my shift and gone home for the evening, feeling a bit guilty for 'recycling' the firearm instead of processing it by the book.

The next morning, I arrived at work and went up to the change room where I was met by a plain-clothes officer, Inspector Decker, and Senior Sergeant Redcliffe. They had my locker open, and inside was the firearm I had given to the other officer. I was asked by Inspector Decker what it was and where it came from. Of course, I lied and said I had never seen it before.

Sergeant Redcliffe said, 'Constable, I saw you with this firearm yesterday. What's it doing in your locker?'

'I have no idea; I didn't put it there,' I replied. Which was true. I gave it to the cop who asked me for it.

Inspector Decker said, 'Well, you're the only one with a key aren't you?'

I said, 'No, I'm not. There are several master keys floating about. They'll open any lock in this joint. You know that.'

'Who's got one of those?' Redcliffe enquired.

'How the fuck would I know? All I know is that they're out there.'

Inspector Decker said, 'I need to see you in my office now.'

We walked down the hallway to Inspector Decker's office. I sat down and he said, 'You're in a bit of trouble young fella!'

'Why?' I asked. 'I didn't steal it!' I knew damn well that I had. I didn't steal it for my own gain but I'd stolen it nonetheless.

Inspector Decker said, 'If you put in your resignation today, I won't bother proceeding with any charges.'

I said, 'Yeah, you'd love that wouldn't you, you big fuck? You've had it in for me since the day I started.'

Decker said, 'Watch your mouth and remember who you're talking to.'

I said, 'I want to speak to my wife. Give me until tomorrow.'

'Ok. I'll expect your resignation on my desk by 9.00 am. I'll change your shift to make sure you're on the morning shift.'

I went home and told Sophie what I had done and what the outcome would be. The consensus was that I should resign, but I wanted to canvass all of my options with a clear head. My head couldn't have been more clouded. I had the stress of the assault, stress of the marriage, and the stress of Sophie not being near her family. I was copping it from all angles. It was one of those times I really needed Jann. She was great to talk to and, no matter what the circumstance, she always made me feel better about myself. That was not an option.

As requested by Inspector Decker, I went into work the next day. I rostered on at 7.00 am for station duty. I worked till 8.00 am, then I walked into the charge room, drew my revolver, and fired one shot into the ceiling. Everyone shit themselves.

I said to the duty sergeant, 'I'm done. Take this before I hurt someone or myself. I'm going home.' I handed him my revolver and walked out of the station, never to return.

I was on stress leave for two months before I landed myself a job as a used car salesman at Pennant Hills Toyota. I couldn't start there until I had finished with the police force.

The next time I saw a police officer was when a sergeant from the Gosford patrol came to the door to collect my uniform and appointments. That was 8 August 1994; the final day of my police career. In summing up my career in the police force, I would have to say that, all in all, it was a traumatic experience. I saw things that folks just ain't meant to see; things that changed me – not for the better. I'm very glad I got out when I did, before it completely broke me.

CHAPTER FOURTEEN

I started my new job as a car salesman, but quickly found that I wasn't shonky enough to sell cars for a living, so I quit after only two weeks. Because of my incapacity to function normally due to post-traumatic stress disorder, I found it hard to find employment that would challenge me enough to take my mind off my worries and off my 'shadow'.

In January, 1996, I got a job as sales manager with a timber flooring company in Willoughby, in Sydney's northern suburbs. I loved working with timber and, although not a hands-on position, I was still attracted to the job at King Cork. Peter Capillos was the owner's name. He was a wealthy businessman who owned several businesses, including a construction company and a pharmacy. A pharmacist by profession, he was the nicest guy, but would only pay me off the books. I didn't like that much, but it did help pay the bills and it wasn't a bad wage for what I did. His brother, Con, was the store manager. Con Capillos from King Cork.

On 16 February 1996, Sophie gave birth to our third, and final, baby, a son we named Matt, after my dad. It seemed fitting, as Dad was a hero of mine. A finer, more ethical and honest man you could not hope to meet. He always used to say to us: 'Kids, always think before you act. If I wouldn't like it, don't do it.' I always took that advice into account. I didn't always follow the advice, but I always thought about it.

Matt's birth was bittersweet for me though, because Dad had this miniature cricket bat signed by an Australian Cricket side. I'm not sure what year it was but the deal was that the firstborn grandson got it. Sasha beat us by six weeks. Bitch! I really wanted that bat for Matt, but it wasn't to be.

I stayed at King Cork for three years, then left to start my own business: 'Nature's Own – Timber Flooring'. This was what I knew. It was my trade. I was very excited because I knew I would make a bit of money out of it. And I did.

One of the first jobs I did in my own business was to install a floor at a shop in a shopping centre in Campbelltown. It had to be done after-hours so I was going to do it on a Sunday. I was travelling down the F3 Freeway from Gosford and was driving across the Hawkesbury River Bridge in the nearside lane when I noticed this huge cruiser about to pass under the bridge. On the front deck were two gorgeous women with long flowing hair, sunbaking topless. I noticed immediately how brown they were against the white fiberglass deck of the cruiser. I wanted to have a real good look at the girls so I lifted my head up in order to see over the guard railing. While I was perving, I didn't notice that there was a car stopped in my lane ahead. Just as they disappeared under the bridge, I turned my eyes back to the road and thought, *Oh crap!*

I reefed the steering wheel to the right but it was too late. I smashed into a Triton Ute that had stopped on the bridge. The Triton flipped over onto its lid and my steering arm snapped so I couldn't steer my truck. In front of the Triton was a LandCruiser towing a horse float with a horse in it. Funnily enough, my truck, steering itself, went around the horse float and smashed into the LandCruiser.

The impact was savage. The damage to all vehicles was extensive and closed the southbound lanes of the F3 for four hours. Luckily, nobody was hurt. The moral of the story is: if you own a multi-million dollar cruiser and you're piloting it up the Hawkesbury, have consideration for the road users using the F3.

It amazes me how many frustrated women there are out there. Men are too stupid to realise that they are neglecting their wives to the point where they are looking for either a 'quickie' to satisfy their fantasy urges, or they are after a long-term affair because their emotional needs are not being met. Either way, I always imagined there must be a big market out there for male escorts. When I thought about it though, maybe it was just impulsiveness on the women's part because they had a nice strapping young man in the house all alone and nobody would notice if they had a fling.

I have to say, that if I wasn't married and I was good-looking and was fit and had a good body, I would have had that much sex with so many different women I could have written a book about that instead. I don't mean to judge these people because they obviously have needs that aren't being met. What I am saying is that, for the most part, women are very emotional and have a greater need for intimacy than men. A man needs to give the woman he loves a reason not to stray. I don't know who authored the theory of monogamy, but I think it's a fallacy. Although in some cases it does work, humans generally find it hard work to love the same person for a life-time. I suppose that the exception is when two people are each others 'One'.

Although I thought that Jann was my 'One', I know that I wasn't hers.

* * * *

At that stage, I didn't know what I wanted to do next, so I decided to start driving tour coaches. See Australia and get paid for it. What a lark!

In 2000, Sophie and I, along with our three kids, moved from Kariong to a house on a one-acre block at Somersby. We had moved from a fairly modern four-bedroom home to a little two-bedroom fibro shack. The plan was to build an enormous country manor.

After driving coaches for other companies, we continued to save so that I could buy my own coach. I continued to learn about the business and see what was involved from a management point of view. I bought my first coach and started 'Zipper Tours' in January 2000.

To start with, I marketed the business around young people. The coach had an esky on board and was a BYO coach. It even had a chute down to a bin below for the patrons to throw their empties. Unfortunately, some people also saw it as a toilet... nice! It was good fun but hard work.

I used to take tours to Fraser Island, Adelaide, Tasmania, Victoria, Brisbane: all over the place. I once took a tour to Tasmania on a fourteen-day trip. We boarded the Spirit of Tasmania in Sydney. I spewed from the time we left Sydney Heads until the next morning when we reached Devonport. I even had to call the ship's plumber to my room to unclog my sink. It was blocked up with my chicken sandwiches from the day before. The sad thing was that the doctor had run out of the shots that stop you throwing up. It was a particularly rough trip and half of the passengers were as crook as Rookwood (that's a cemetery in Sydney).

There is one thing I will never do if I get back into coach driving. I will never work with seniors' groups again. The politics of who gets to sit where and on what day, and some passengers not speaking to others because they took their seat; it was alarming. So much for maturity.

Another funny thing is that, as you get older, apparently you just don't give a shit if, or where, you drop a dirty great fart. Old people just accept it as the 'done' thing. You're in a quiet area of some display and suddenly – riiiiiiiiip. Old Betsy lets one loose which, in turn, starts a chain reaction. You just don't want to be around when that happens. It's disturbing!

Then there's the toilet on the coach. I thought women were supposed to be refined and fairly well contained down there. How a woman can go to the toilet and come out followed by a stream of urine is beyond me. NO MORE SENIORS TRIPS.....EVER!

It was great fun for most of the time though, because I got in to all of the attractions for free and I saw some really interesting stuff. But I did miss being at home a lot. The longest time I was away was seventeen days and that almost killed me. I used to get plenty of offers from the ladies on the tours; however, none were worth losing my marriage over. Well, some might have been – I will never know.

There was one time when I took a charter group to the Hunter Valley Winery on a hens' night. We did the usual winery tour circuit and then I dropped them at Harrigan's Irish Pub. It was around dusk at the time. There was one girl, about twenty-three years old at a guess, who kept smiling at me and brushing up against me as she got on and off the bus. She wasn't a 'bad sort' by any means but I wasn't sure what was going on. I didn't know if she was drunk, or just into me. Possibly the former. After all, I'm no oil painting.

I had dropped the ladies off at Harrigan's and I got back onto the bus and just pulled the door closed. It wasn't locked, but that didn't worry me because I was on it. I took a pillow with me so I could have a little nap. I was stretched out on the back seat of the coach with the curtains drawn. I heard the door open and felt the slight weight shift as someone entered the coach, but I thought it was one of the girls who had forgotten something, so I didn't worry about it. I had a quick peek, saw this nice female form silhouetted against the street light, and closed my eyes again. A few moments later, I heard the girl walking towards me, so I thought she must have needed something at the back of the coach. Apparently she did ... me.

It was Miss Twenty-three. She went down on her knees and tried to unzip my pants. I stopped her. She had her top completely unbuttoned and no bra on. For a thirty-five year old man to see a thing of beauty kneeling before him with breasts that you could only dream about was heart-wrenching. She put my hand on her breast and tried to unzip my pants again. I stopped her again. I knew that if she were to get her hands on me, I would be gone.

I said to her, 'I can't, I'm sorry.'

She asked, 'Why not, don't you like me?'

I said, 'I don't know you. I am married. Don't do this. I'm sorry. Can you please get dressed and leave the coach.'

She pleaded, 'I won't tell anyone ... Please?'

'In another life maybe but, if I got caught, it would definitely be in another life.'

'Ok, your loss.'

I have no doubt that, in one respect, she was right. It was a loss but one I could live with. She had the body of a goddess. For all I knew, it could have been a dare from the other girls. I don't know. Fun to fantasise about though. I'm probably the only straight man on earth who would have knocked that back.

When the girls started getting back on the coach, I moved back up to the driver's seat. Miss Twenty-three got back on the coach and gave me the biggest smile. I returned the compliment. Customer service took on a whole new meaning for me that night, but it was one occasion in which the customer wasn't always right ... for me, anyway.

When I dropped them off in the early hours of the morning, Miss Twenty-three gave me a kiss on the cheek on the way off the coach, smiled, and said, 'See you in the afterlife.' I just laughed.

Although I loved working on the coach tours, I didn't like being away from home, so I decided to sell the business. It didn't take long before it was snapped up by a young fella wanting the lifestyle that I had built up. I had also built the timber flooring business up into a nice money-earner until I sold it in 2001. Another chapter in my life was at an end.

* * * *

In January, 2002, Sophie and I went on a skiing holiday to Whistler in Canada. It was like a winter wonderland and, if you love the snow, in my opinion, it is the only place on earth. Pure magic! I was in the advanced ski group, even though I was an intermediate skier. I like to challenge myself at everything I do and skiing was no exception. One night, they had an awards night to give out fun awards to those who had performed well and to those who had done some silly things. I was the only person to receive two awards on the night. One, which I was most pleased about, was the fastest time completing the slalom course, even though I was the only person ever to win it while crossing the finish line on his arse. Why turn? It only slows you down.

The second award was for the most unusual descent over a drop-off. I attempted to follow the instructor but went a little wide off the mark. I hit a tree branch, which threw me out of my skis and down the face of the drop-off. As I saw my skis overtake me down the face, I tried to speed up and I actually started to try and swim. They said it looked really funny and, for that, I deserved the award which, to me, looked like a sexual aid for women, which I mentioned to rapturous laughter. It was actually a massage device ... so they say. I still haven't worked out how to use it, other than for what I originally thought it was for.

While we were there, we flew over to New York for five days, which isn't nearly enough time. New York is probably one of my favourite places that I've ever been to. So much to see, so much to do. We did the romantic horse and cart ride through Central Park. We went up to the top of the Empire State Building and, yes, Sophie did say that she was either waiting for Tom Hanks or King Kong. Cheesy! I knew it was Tom she was waiting for.

We visited the site of the 911 terrorist attacks. It was very emotional. The area of destruction was immense. The damage to adjoining buildings was catastrophic and the tributes that were left on a daily basis were very moving. I took a number of NSW Police Badges to give to NYPD patrol officers as mementoes for the good work they do.

I love the restaurants in New York, but you don't have to be Einstein to know why Americans have an obesity problem. The food over there is amazing; not only the quality, but the quantity on your plate. You will never leave a restaurant hungry in New York.

After we left a restaurant one evening and were trying to find our way around, I saw a lady standing by a building, so I approached her to ask for directions. As I walked towards her, she looked me in the eye and started backing away. I said, 'It's alright, I'm not going to hurt you, I just need directions.' She smiled and had a look of relief on her face. It's sad to think that people should fear being alone, even in a crowded street.

If there's one thing I would take out of New York and bring to Australia, it's their zero tolerance for crime. When walking through Central Park, even at night, there were single women walking their dogs, jogging, and so on. I felt very safe. There were police everywhere. It was very reassuring. A complete contradiction to the reaction from the lady in the street. The only time I didn't feel safe was on the subway. Sophie and I caught the ferry over to New Jersey to see my cousin, Kayla, who married an American lawyer. We had dinner with them and then caught the ferry back. When we jumped on the train it was full. As we travelled up town it started to empty. By the time it had reached the stop before ours, everybody was gone except us and one very dodgy-looking character at the end of the carriage. I looked at him and he looked at me. I stuck my chest out and sat up straight and tried to make myself look as big as possible. Nothing happened, of course, but I know how the lady on the street must have felt when she had a dodgy-looking bloke walking towards her.

I then got on the phone to Vancouver as I wanted to book tickets to see an ice hockey game. You can't go to Canada and not see an ice hockey game. It was just after 911, so security was really tight. We had excellent tickets halfway along, about ten rows back. I took my video camera out and started to film the game. A security officer rushed over to me and told me I couldn't film the game for security reasons. I asked him if I could take stills and he said that was ok. Anyway, I thought I'd wait until the last quarter and film that, so I waited patiently. After what I thought was the third quarter ended, 'WE WON' came up on the big screen.

Ice hockey is played in thirds. Foiled again! A funny thing occurs during the game though. When a player gets a hat-trick, everybody in the crowd throws their hat onto the ice and they have to stop the game to pick them up. They then get donated to charity. It's a nice idea.

After we returned from our holiday, something occurred to me. I had just been halfway around the world with my wife on the holiday of a lifetime and I wouldn't have wanted to do it with anyone else. I love my wife.

* * * *

After we got home, I noticed that the neighbour was building an animal pen right on our boundary. I didn't ask him what it was. I thought I'd wait and see. A bloody pig pen. Several weeks after the pigs moved in, the smell became quite disturbing. I asked my neighbour if he could move the pen and he said 'No'. This became a running battle between us, as I had rung the local council. They told him that, even though it was in a rural area, it was too close to our house and he would have to do something about it. He did.

He erected the most hideous-looking corrugated iron fence. It was supposed to serve two purposes but only served one. It was supposed to filter the smell when the wind blew in our direction. It didn't. It was supposed to look ugly just to piss me off. It did that all right. I asked him to pull it down on several occasions and he refused. I then checked the property alignments and saw that he had built the fence one foot on my side of the boundary. I then gave him a choice: either he moved it or I would. He refused.

I was at work a couple of weeks later and decided to leave early. I was going home to chop this fence down. I got home, grabbed my axe, and started destroying the fence. The next thing I knew, the police were on my doorstep. The neighbour came out with a big smile on his face saying that he'd moved the fence during the day. I checked the boundary peg and he was correct. The police informed me that they were going to charge me with malicious damage to the fence.

I was ashamed. I would be the first person in our family ever to get charged with a criminal offence. I was also determined to be the first person to get off. I went to the library in Gosford and investigated the offence itself and any possible defenses. Bingo! I had what I needed.

In court, I noticed that my opponent for the day, the police prosecutor, was an ex-Parramatta football great. I told the magistrate that I had video evidence I needed to present and he informed me that the courtroom had no facilities to view it. He directed the prosecutor to view the tape to see what the evidence was. After viewing the tape, the prosecutor told me that, despite my evidence, he was going to proceed.

I said, 'Neville, I'm going to kick your arse, mate.'

He looked at me and said, 'I do this for a living. We'll see whose arse gets kicked.'

We made our way back to the courtroom and proceedings got underway. After the prosecutor had presented his case, it was my turn in defense. I simply said to the magistrate, 'Sir, I believed that I had the right to remove the fence because, at the time I attempted to remove it, I thought it was on my property.'

The prosecutor got to his feet and attempted to say something, but the magistrate put his hand up to stop him talking. He had his head down for a moment in deep thought. He looked up and said, 'The one and only defense to malicious damage is that the accused is of the belief that they had the right to commit the act. In this case, given the evidence provided, I am of the opinion that, at the time of the act of cutting down the fence, Mr Walton was of the belief that the fence was still on his property. Therefore, I find the offence not proved and I am dismissing the case.'

The prosecutor wasn't happy. Outside the courthouse, I simply said to him, 'Told you I'd kick your arse.'

He didn't reply. That's one thing I love about being an ex-cop. I know what's required to get out of a tricky situation.

It wasn't long after that that we put the Somersby house on the market. We had the plans for the 'manor' drawn up; however, things started to sour. I was working in Sydney at the time and it was really getting to Sophie. It had also become a real chore to drive from Somersby to Gosford every day, several times a day, so I made the decision to move back to Kariong until the kids were old enough to fend for themselves.

Sophie was upset to be leaving. She is very much a homemaker. I see a house as just that ... a house. She sees the home between the walls; the people in it, the hard work that went into making that little fibro cottage into a home. The barbecues with friends, the bonfires we used to have and the fireworks that went with them, and the morning after ... cooking damper in the ashes with the kids. Sophie sees all of that. I see bricks and mortar.

It didn't take long to sell because it was a beautiful block of land. When we bought it, it was an acre of bindi-eye and rubbish. We removed over ten tons of crap. When we left, it was like parkland. Absolutely beautiful. We had been at Somersby for two years and, in that time, we had nearly doubled our money on the block. I had also purchased a studio apartment in Potts Point and sold that for a good profit, and then a two-bedroom unit in Gosford which I also sold for a tidy profit twelve months later.

We moved back to Kariong and bought another house. The couple next door were getting a divorce so we bought their house as well. I love real estate. Buy well and you can't go wrong. Unfortunately, sometimes people make a fortune out of other people's misfortune.

* * * *

Again, I wanted to do something I had never done before. I saw an ad in the newspaper seeking parking rangers with Pittwater Council. I gave it a burl and got the gig. Although similar to the police, it's not rocket science to write a parking ticket or a ticket for an unleashed dog. I was given a car to drive around in, I was in the sun and fresh air, and the northern beaches of Sydney is one of the most beautiful places around.

We used to go up to Palm Beach and watch them shooting episodes of *Home and Away*. Every now and again we'd have a bit of fun and write tickets for the cast members' cars. It was an inventive way to meet them, as they would always track us down and have a carry-on about it. We always used to cancel the tickets for them, but then we could chat and get autographs for our kids, and so on. For the record, Lyn McGrainger is a darling. She has a fan in me.

Because I spent a lot of time walking around Palm Beach, I had a lot of time to think about my life and what might have been if things had been different. What would I be doing if I didn't have Sophie? What if I had met someone else? I thought about Jann a lot as well. My memories of her were still as vivid as if I had only seen her yesterday. Only I knew. The only reality check that I kept coming back to was that I knew that, if I saw her today, she would look different. It had been seventeen years since I had last seen Jann, but I still always wondered what might have been.

Because of my police experience, I was selected to become a trainer for the new parking officers. You could always tell the officers that I'd trained. They were always fair but firm. A few of us used to have a competition to see who could write the most tickets in a shift. I was generally the quickest but couldn't crack the 100-a-day mark. I think the highest anybody got was 121 for a shift. That was on a New Year's Day at Palm Beach.

I went to work one day and was rostered on with a new guy I was training up. Tecki was his name. He seemed like a nice enough guy, but there was something odd about him. We were working in Avalon when I noticed a motorist park his BMW on a pedestrian crossing. I couldn't see him so I wrote him a ticket. He returned and drove off before I could place the ticket on his windscreen. I left it in the book so I could send it to him in the post.

About five minutes later, I saw him again stopping in front of the same pedestrian crossing waiting for people to cross. I approached his car and attempted to pass the ticket to him through his passenger-side window. He didn't take it so I dropped it in. He got out of his car and approached me very aggressively and pushed me to the ground. I got up and he grabbed my shirt. This guy was strong. We started wrestling. I called to Tecki to come and help me.

I kept trying to get Tecki to come over. I saw him looking over but he didn't attempt to help me. After what seemed an eternity, I broke free of the motorist. I didn't chase him as I was spent. At that stage, Tecki came over to me and helped me pick my things up off the road. I went to the police station to report the incident and then I went to the doctor.

Tecki came up to me later on and said, 'I hope this doesn't affect our working relationship.'

I said, 'Tecki, it won't, because I'll be recommending that you be dismissed. What you did was nothing short of cowardly; to watch a workmate getting overpowered and to do nothing. You and I are done.'

I saw my boss the next day and told her that I would never work with Tecki again. Following my grievance, he was dismissed that day. Again, I asked myself what I did wrong. Could I have done anything differently? Perhaps I should have just sent the motorist the ticket in the mail. I only stayed in that job for eighteen months but I did like it. After that assault at Avalon, too many memories came flooding back, so I left.

* * * *

My mate Thomas, from the Chinatown restaurant incident, and his family moved to the Central Coast from Taree. He sold his mechanical business and bought a construction company. Over the next couple of years, he and his wife Georgi, rebuilt the company into a very profitable and respected company. I often joke that everything Thomas touches turns to gold. But it's the hard work that he puts into it that makes the gold. He is literally, the hardest working person I have ever known. I respect him for that.

I have this theory that straight men and women can never really be friends. Given the right set of circumstances, a bloke would 'boof' a girl without giving it a second thought. Georgi is different. I really do consider her a mate in her own right. She is the most forthright and honest person I know and she could easily stand alongside my dad and my wife in the same category. I love her to death: she is one awesome woman. It doesn't matter how much shit I give her. She always hits back. I love that about her. She has a great sense of humour and is as smart as all get out.

Thomas is one of those accident-prone guys who loves anything that is fast but, really, should just be watching it on TV. On my thirtieth birthday, he snapped his hip travelling at over 160 km/h bare foot waterskiing. He eventually had to have a hip replacement as a result of a botched operation. It took years for Thomas to be fit enough to start enjoying life again. We started to get back into dirt bike riding. We used to do it as teenagers back in Taree. My son and Thomas's three boys really loved camping with us, as did Thomas's mate, Droopy, and his family.

Dirt biking demands respect for each other, the machines, and the bush. While Thomas was riding in the bush, he came off his bike and broke two vertebrae in his back, and Georgi had to wipe his bum for the next three months. Then, twelve months after that, at a place called Louee, at Mudgee, on his first ride back, he flew over the handlebars and broke his collarbone. I mean, really; the biggest bike he should be riding is one bolted to a carrousel at a carnival. Having said that, he can really ride. He likes to have a go at everything. If it's got a motor, Thomas is good at it. He used to drive a rally car at one stage. He asked me to co-drive but I get motion-sickness if I try to read in a car, so trying to read pace notes at 180 km/h was never going to work. Again, he was successful at that as well. Whatever he has a go at, he puts in 100 per cent. I admire him for that.

* * * *

As time has marched on, the kids have grown up and have developed other interests, so the camping trips have become fewer and further between, which is a shame. I love the solitude, the comradery and the time to forget about my 'shadow' – even just for a short while.

In 2005, we moved again, this time from Kariong to Green Point, also on the Central Coast. I wanted something to keep me busy so I bought a concrete truck. Everyone was telling me that concrete trucks were a license to print money. Bullshit! I only had the concrete truck for two years. I think my PTSD had a lot to do with it because I had a very short fuse and don't suffer fools lightly and, in the concreting industry, there are a lot of fools.

I was standing on the back of the truck at a job one day and there was a blockage in the concrete pump. The dickhead at the end of the pump didn't just clear the blockage, he decided to show me the piece of crap up close, from thirty metres away. He threw the piece of dried concrete at me and I wasn't expecting it. It hit me in the eye. I had safety glasses on, but the force of it shattered the glasses and gave me a big cut around the eye. I got the shits and left the site to get medical attention.

I went back to the yard to clean out the truck. The boss – another Con – got into me for leaving a site with concrete in the barrel. I told him to fuck off and left. That was ultimately 'the straw that broke the camel's back'. There were other incidences, but that definitely was the worst. I kept the concrete truck for two years before selling it and buying a pallet manufacturing plant.

Pallets – how exciting … NOT! But business has always been exciting to me. I love the challenge of exceeding the expectations of my clients, as well as expanding the business into new markets and finding new clients. I wouldn't care if it was ladies' underwear or mining equipment. The products change but the principles stay the same, more or less.

I bought it as a run-down concern with the intention of building it up and selling it after twelve months. The first thing I did was trim costs where necessary and look at pricing. After a rationalisation program, the business was where I wanted it to be. I was always striving to source new customers and new suppliers. I accepted the challenge and conquered it. It's not my theory, but, it's one I subscribe to…It's better to save a dollar than it is to make a dollar. For every dollar you make, you pay tax on it. For every dollar you save, you pay no tax at all. It's an easy principle to grasp but most businesses don't utilise the strategy and I don't understand why. It's ok to keep increasing your turnover, but as you do that, your tax liability increases. Reduce your expenses and you increase your profit and pay no extra tax.

The business was going very well but soon I could sense a change in the ordering pattern of some of my clients. Not always bad changes, but changes just the same. I had the business on the market for three months with a broker who had delivered me no enquiries. At that stage, I had an idea. Instead of selling the company as a whole, I decided to break it up into two regions, Sydney and Central Coast – Newcastle.

I started to direct market to other pallet manufacturers in the hope that one or two of them would want to buy a new customer base. Mine was extensive and I knew it would prove lucrative to anyone in the industry. I had the Sydney region sold within a week and the Central Coast – Newcastle region within a month. Mission accomplished. Bloody brokers! I hate incompetence. Why should I pay them a commission after doing their job for them.

From January 2010, I had a break from work for a period of six months. I eventually got a job as the manager of a tyre shop on the Central Coast. The first thing I wanted to do was to build the mechanical side of the business to grow the customer base and increase turnover. The second thing was to cut cost, which were extensive to say the least.

It was apparent though that the business had a reputation in the area that was less than ideal so I attempted to change the perception of the shop and that was hard work. It was evident though that the shop was on a downhill slide.

* * * *

Thomas's family and ours went to New Zealand on a holiday and we decided to visit the South Island, as Sophie and I had already travelled the North Island twice previously. We did all the extreme stuff like swimming with the seals, whitewater rafting, and the ultimate … skydiving.

We walked into the shop front in Queenstown to book our tickets. Only Erik, our godson, Siion, Matt, and I were going to do it. I have an inherent fear of heights so just the thought of it was scary. We were in the shop and we had to hop on the scales. The limit was 100 kilograms. Everyone was under that weight but me. I weighed in at 105 kilograms. I was on holidays and wasn't watching the calories – not that I ever did. Anyway, I told the lady I needed to do it with my kids but she was adamant. I started to strip off in the shop with total strangers looking on in the hope of shedding the excess kilo's required. The girl behind the counter started to laugh. I stripped down to my undies and was still overweight by 2 kilograms.

I said to the shop attendant, 'I know these undies don't weigh two kilos but, in the interest of getting on that plane, I'm willing to find out. Are you?'

She told me to hang on. She made a phone call to the jumpmaster and he agreed that, given what I was threatening to do, he would allow me to go. I didn't know if I was happy or stupid. Stupid was the correct answer.

The next day, we all went to the aerodrome and signed in. I got buddied with this huge Croatian dude. We all got into the plane and I was the last one in. We sat on the floor and I was right in front of the perspex door. It closed automatically. From where I sat, I could see straight through it. As the plane accelerated, it hit home that there was no turning back. If I didn't go, nobody else would be going, as I was blocking the door.

As we climbed towards the 9000-feet ceiling, I was looking at my daughter, Siion. I must have looked a sight. I took her by the hand and mouthed to her, 'I'm shitting myself'. She and her jump buddy laughed. As we reached the ceiling, the pilot cut back the engine, leveled the plane and the perspex door just slid open in front of me. I swear I almost soiled myself there and then. I felt my jump buddy's legs wrap around me and he pushed me towards the door until my legs were dangling outside the plane. I looked down and thought, *Fuck me!*

My jump buddy said loudly, 'Do you want me to count down, or just go?'

Just as I was about to answer, he pushed.

I immediately felt my stomach go light and we twisted and I saw the plane flying away. We flipped back over and I saw the most beautiful scenery I had ever seen. We were freefalling for about a minute. It was the best thing I had ever done. Janelle can eat her heart out. Apart from when I nearly shit myself on the plane, this was better than sex. I could see the ground rushing up toward me and all I could do was hope like hell that I was strapped in and the chute opened.

My buddy tapped me on the shoulder to let me know he was about to pull the cord. When he did, it was like getting hit with a sledgehammer. The thud was massive but, straight after … total silence. Just a whisper of wind through my ever-thinning hair. It was so peaceful.

It's at times like this that you really start to question your purpose in life. Here I am, dangling by two cords from a glorified bed sheet 6,000 feet above the ground. There wasn't a cloud in the sky. The air was crisp and clean. Apart from the sheer scenic beauty of Queenstown, I thought to myself, *Many people before me have done exactly the same thing…and died.* As thrilling as the freefall was, I couldn't wait to get my feet back on terra firma.

On the ground, I didn't know what to do, so I watched my son, my daughter, and my godson touch down safely. I ran over and gave each of them a big hug. I was so proud of them. The courage they showed at such a young age was mind-blowing. I admire all three of them. Skydiving really challenges your inner self. You may have a fear of it at the beginning, but once you have done it, it is one of the most exhilarating things you will ever do in your life. Yet it doesn't have to be skydiving. Confront your fear and kick it in the balls. You will be a better person for it.

Although everything else paled into insignificance compared to the skydiving, I loved the whitewater rafting. Not because of the rush that I'd get but because Sophie had a go. She's not a real water person and hates putting her head under the water, so the thought of falling out must have terrified her. I could see the concern on her face as we got closer to getting into the raft. I let the guide know about her concerns and so he placed her right beside him so she felt safe. I wanted to go right up the front where the action was. It was a great experience but wasn't as rough as

I would have liked it. But from Sophie's point of view, it was just fine.

After it was over, I could see the relief on Sophie's face. I was so proud of her that day.

We decided to go paintballing on the final day. It was Thomas and his two boys against Matt, Siion, and me. I wanted to split the teams so there'd be no inter-family rivalry. That didn't wash with Thomas. Thomas has been known to be 'a little competitive' when it comes to our families. He wanted to have family against family and so, that's what happened.

Anybody who has ever played paintball will know that, when you get hit, it bloody well hurts. The game began. The setting was bush; as realistic as jungle warfare would get I'd say. We were dressed in our greens and hiding as best we could. Siion was hiding in between some tyres. She was our last line of defense stopping our enemy from capturing our bell. I had no idea where Matt was. I went straight up the middle of the field, hid under a bush, and waited.

Hee, hee, hee. Sure enough, along came Thomas walking straight towards me. I was sure he'd spot me but I was well hidden. I could see one of his team holding position at their bell but I couldn't see the other. As Thomas approached, I opened fire when he was about ten metres away. He put his hands in the air to signal that he was out and walked off the battlefield. I couldn't believe that he was right in front of me and still didn't see me. What I also couldn't believe was that his son, who was guarding their bell, did see me and opened fire. I could hear pellets zipping past me everywhere when, eventually, clunk. I was hit, fair in the head. What a great shot! He was well over fifty metres away.

When Thomas and I re-entered the game, it was on. I went straight for their bell and he went straight for ours. We both got hit again but I wasn't having any of that. I just opened fire on 'em. Even after I was hit, I just claimed it was a minor flesh wound. It got to a point where Erik did the best job of not being seen. It was right at the end when he shot me right in the guts. I was supposed to be out but, again, I couldn't help myself. I shot him a couple of times and then peppered Thomas. To say that they were displeased would be an understatement. My troupe and I high tailed it out of there back to base camp where our wives were waiting.

Thomas was whinging like a big sook but, due to an indiscretion he committed against me earlier in the trip, I had to hit back. I was just biding my time. Payback is a bitch. Thomas knows that whatever he does to me will be returned threefold. I think he enjoys trying to work out what I'll come up with.

Before we headed back to the hotel, Siion and I went horse-riding. It was a really relaxing afternoon considering the intense morning. Sophie stayed in the motorhome reading a book. I'm not the best with horses but for Siion … anything. It was a great father/daughter moment.

The next day, we flew back into Sydney. I love going on holidays but I also love getting home. We caught the train back from the airport and were just sitting quietly when Thomas said, 'We'll have to do that again soon.'

'No,' was my simple response.

Although it was a great trip and we did plenty of exiting things, we also had some tense moments between us when our friends wanted to do one thing and we wanted to do another. On a couple of occasions we did our own thing, but that's not what the trip was about. Anyway, my advice is this: don't go on holidays with people you want to stay friends with.

CHAPTER FIFTEEN

Although I feel that I am on top of it, I still suffer from debilitating bouts of depression. At times, I have thought that it would be so easy to go to the gun cabinet, take out a 'shotty', and put a dirty great hole in my chest. I'd never do a headshot. I'm too considerate. After being in the police and seeing the result, nobody would do that to themselves knowing what their family had to see when they're done. It's not like in the movies when someone gets shot in the head and there's a nice little hole and a bit of blood. When someone shoots themselves in the head, the bullet goes in and out quickly, but the gasses enter the skull and expand rapidly. Basically they explode your head to the point where you are unrecognisable to all but the dentist and pathologist.

I have even got to the point where I have written five 'goodbye' letters: one to my wife, one to each of my three children, and one to Jann. They remain buried within my computer, as one never knows if, or when, they will be needed.

The trouble I have with killing myself is that I have people around me who love me and rely on me. If they weren't around, there would be no point to me being here. But they are around, so I have to put up with my pain for them. Therefore, I gladly shoulder the burden, as heavy as it has become. Everyone has their breaking point. I just haven't reached mine yet. I suspect that, given that I suffer from mental illness, it could happen one day … any day.

Every now and again, I think of Jann. When I knew her all those years ago, I didn't have any worries. We were just carefree young pups having a great time. She was always happy, which made me happy. To this day I still think about what went wrong with our relationship. It is a bittersweet feeling because I should be happy enough with the woman I love now; the woman I am married to; the mother of my three beautiful kids. Sometimes, when things just aren't going your way, it's just easier to live in fantasyland.

* * * *

My kids, in particular my daughters, were hounding me to connect to Facebook on the internet. On 10 December 2011, Siion connected me and I just let it sit there. I wasn't really interested in it but, one day, I was bored and decided to have a go.

I did what I thought any normal bloke would do … I did a search for my ex. I found a photo of her now. I wasn't 100 per cent sure it was her but she looked too good not to be. I sent her a short but quirky message which read, 'Hi Jann, just wondering if it's you.' Then I followed it up quickly with, 'Probably not, you look too good to be my Jann.'

There was no answer for a while and I forgot about the message I had sent. Maybe it wasn't her. A month later I received a message back: 'Yes, Mitch, I think I am the Jann you're looking for. I think that was meant to be a compliment and, as the years are getting on, I'll take it as one.'

You have no idea how I felt after she replied to my message. It was as if my depressed state just disappeared. I was instantly happier within myself.

The messages started to flow back and forth quite innocently. We started to talk about what we had been doing for the past twenty-odd years. I remembered Jann as a girl who thrived on sitting down and talking about her deepest feelings and darkest secrets. I remember once we sat on Cronulla Beach and talked for hours about life, love, and other such mysteries.

She told me that she had been married for twenty-three years, same as me. She was currently living in Brisbane. She had two daughters. She had left nursing and had owned a café for the past three years. Up until recently, we had had a border collie named Tom; she had two border collies. The only difference between our circumstances really, was that her house was ultra-modern. Ours was ultra-old and I had a son.

As our conversations got deeper, I became more guarded. I asked Siion about Facebook security. She became suspicious and did a search on me.

'Who's Jann _ _ _ _ _ _?' she asked very loudly.

I saw Sophie's head come popping around the corner of the dining room where she was doing some school work. I thought to myself, *Fuck me! Here we go.*

'That's his ex-girlfriend who he wanted to marry,' she said.

Siion replied, 'Oh yeah, she's quite pretty.'

I said, 'Yes, she is.'

Sophie said, 'Are you Facebook friends with her?'

I said, 'Yeah.'

You see, Sophie had asked me to be her friend on Facebook and I had said 'No'. I didn't know what she could see and I didn't want her to see what was being written between Jann and me. I considered our communication was private and I wanted it to stay that way.

CHAPTER SIXTEEN

It had taken all of two minutes to start stirring up the old feelings that I had for Jann. She then started telling me about things that had occurred within her marriage that would have destroyed most peoples'. My reactions to her revelations weren't what she was expecting and she was surprised. The things she told me didn't surprise me in the least. You see, I still think nobody knows Jann better than me. Even she was surprised that I could remember so much about her emotional needs, wants, and desires.

What I couldn't believe was that she had an affair while she and Ashley were engaged and then another one after they got married. The latter affair lasted for sixteen years. Ashley knew about it for most of that time, but decided it was best to share her rather than not have her at all. This is the type of spell that Jann can cast over a man. I'm not passing judgment on Ashley. I think he must really love Jann to stick with her.

Although our contact stirred up the old feelings that I'd had for Jann, I realised that she didn't have the same feelings for me. She made it quite clear that she was happily married and didn't want to go down the path of deceit again. I told her that was ok but I still had very strong feelings for her. She couldn't understand how, after all these years, I could still be in love with her. I told her I didn't know why.

She probed, putting different hypotheses to me as to why I felt the way I did. Her main theory was that I was in love with the memory of her. I think, in hindsight, that may very well be the case, but I dismissed that because it didn't suit my agenda. Plus, the fact that she was my first real girlfriend and first lover played a big part in how I felt about her.

One day, we were chatting and I told her that, over the past nineteen years, I kept having this recurring dream about her. I said, 'Jann, it's quite sexual in nature. Are you sure you want me to tell you?'

She said, 'Yeah, why not?'

I knew then that an important line was about to be crossed.

I told her that I'd write it down and send it to her email address. I didn't hear from her for a couple of hours. Then I heard my phone buzz. The message read, 'I'm all snuggled up in bed. How about sending me that dream?'

I replied, 'Ok, here it comes.' I pressed send. It was the dream on the train.

A reply came about eight minutes later. 'Oh my God! Where did you learn to write like that?' she asked. 'Is that what I've been missing all these years? Is that what someone else has been getting? I couldn't help myself. Thanks for the wet spot. Night.'

I had to laugh. She was never one to hold back with her feelings. That's why I love her. If nothing else, we are a perfect match in the emotions department.

I now knew what Jann thought of the dream I'd had about her, but I was really interested to know what Sophie would think. I got on the computer and changed the names from Jann to Sophie. I printed it off and gave it to Sophie to read. I made her think that I wrote it as an exercise in erotic writing. I honestly thought she would get turned on by it and maybe we could have an early night. After all, from Jann's reply, just her response was enough to turn me on. Unfortunately, Sophie told me she thought it was smut, although she did say she thought that it was well written. It wasn't what I wanted to hear and it made me want Jann even more.

I think that was the turning point in the situation – where the conversations between Jann and me changed from ex-partners to potential lovers ... again. Both of us knew that we would never leave our present partners, but we were tempted by the forbidden fruit and the curiosity and desire that we had re-created in each other's minds.

Given that I could sense that she was into me as much as I was into her, I sent her an email that would leave her in no doubt as to how I felt about her: 'One thing I have always been aware about you and me. Never, not even when we were going out, did you ever tell me you loved me. I promise you this, Jann. It is my mission, not only to get you to say you love me but, by the end of this, you will fall in love with me.'

She replied, 'I fear that may already be happening.'

I could feel her passion for me returning: the passion I'd felt when we were together so long ago. I said to her, 'Jann, one day, we will be together. You will be by my side. I know this because I have a plan.'

'What is your plan?' she enquired.

I told her, 'Women are supposed to live longer than men, right? Well, my plan is to outlive Ashley. I'll give you as much time to grieve as you need, say, two days, and then I'm going to come calling.'

Always the practical one, she replied, 'Mmm, sounds like a plan. But what happens if Sophie is still alive?'

I said, 'We'll cross that bridge when we come to it. It's a long way off yet, unless Ashley gets hit by a bus.'

She said, 'I'll be waiting.'

Our conversations were full of 'what ifs' and 'buts' and other such scenarios. It was fantasy gone mad. But do you know what? It made me feel great.

Sophie has an uncanny knack of knocking romance on the head and, with Jann, it rekindled the passion within me. Jann is the most passionate woman I have ever known. The sex, the intimacy, the emotional connection we felt when we were together; I will never forget that and, maybe, that's what I am actually in love with.

I asked Jann to create a fantasy for me but she explained that she loved reading it but couldn't write it. It made her blush, she said. I was disappointed. She asked me for another one so I said I needed some inspiration. 'Name a place you like to run,' I said.

She said, 'I like to jog along the Port Macquarie break-wall. It's a lovely part of the world.'

I told her that I'd get to work on it right away. I knew it would be a little bit more difficult than the last one, because that one was based on an actual dream that I had over many years. I could recall that dream intimately. This fantasy would have to be based on desire and imagination. The desire I had plenty of but I have the imagination of a house brick.

While all of this was going on, Sophie was getting a bit suspicious about how much time I was spending in front of the TV, yet constantly checking my iPhone. I just told her that it was either eBay enquiries or the odd message from Jann. By this stage, I began to realise that I was in deep. All of those old feelings had come flooding back: that feeling of butterflies whenever I thought of her and the fact that I now thought of Jann more than I thought about my Sophie. It was really getting out of control and the confusion in my mind was sending me bonkers.

I sent Jann the second fantasy message and she almost went ballistic.

* * * *

I went up to Mum and Dad's holiday unit at Port Macquarie. It was in the middle of summer. It was a beautiful day – thirty-two degrees, with a slight breeze blowing across the water. It was 6.30 pm and I decided to go for a walk along the break-wall. Sophie was asleep. I left her a note on the kitchen table, grabbed an ice-cream, and started my stroll. The sea was angry that day. Salt spray drifted gently over the break-wall as the waves crashed onto the rocks. Rainbows danced in the sky as the dimming sunlight shone through the mist.

I got to the end of the wall which was, by now, almost devoid of walkers, and a feeling of loneliness came over me. I took a seat on a rock and watched the waves crashing relentlessly below me. Tiny crabs clung onto anything they could to stop themselves being washed away by the savage motion of the rough seas. As I was looking out to sea contemplating life's challenges, I heard the voice of a woman behind me.

'Beautiful, isn't it?'

I turned and looked up at her. She was silhouetted against the afternoon sun and her curvaceous figure was clearly visible as her free-flowing frock fluttered in the breeze, filtering the light of the sun as it shifted around her body. It was like I had x-ray vision. 'It certainly is,' I replied. We were both talking about different things.

'Would you like to join me, Jann?'

You didn't say anything. You took my hand and I steadied you as you climbed down onto the rock on which I was seated. You sat close beside me and cuddled up to me as though seeking protection from the savage sea. You asked, 'How did you know it was me?'

'Nobody else has a voice that sexy,' I said. You just giggled like a little girl. 'I didn't think I'd see you again after that night on the train.'

'What night on the train?'

'Don't worry, I was thinking of a dream I had,' I replied, laughing to myself. 'You were pretty hot that night, Jann. I see nothing has changed.' We turned to each other and I said, 'You look beautiful.'

Memories came flooding back to me as I looked into your stunningly soulful eyes. You leant over and kissed me. Again, in my mind, I started to question myself. I couldn't understand. *Why is it*, I thought, *that we are so passionate yet we cannot be together?* A question best left unanswered for now.

It was a beautiful kiss; soft, moist, inviting. Just as I'd remembered. I was thinking to myself, *This could be fun but rather uncomfortable*. Nothing could be further from the truth.

The air temperature had dropped slightly. My temperature, however, was rapidly rising. The sun was going down now; only ambient sunlight graced the sky above us. The first stars had begun to appear and the channel marker lights had come on: a green starboard marker, a red port marker, and a white light to alert nighttime mariners of the presence of the break-wall – plus a couple of wayward lovers. It was at that moment that I noticed that the sea had now subsided, reduced to a gentle lapping at the edge of the rocks, and the breeze had dropped. The setting was perfect.

I knew you were concerned about being seen, so I climbed up further onto the rocks and had a look around. We were alone. I came back down to our rock. It was like sitting on piece of volcanic rock; the heat of the sun trapped within, yet radiating into our bodies as we lay down together.

I removed my shirt, folded it, and placed it under your head. Your smile was so beautiful. As I kissed you, I knew that I wouldn't be able to control myself. You ran your fingers through the hair on my chest, which felt really good. I slowly unbuttoned the front of your dress while gazing into your eyes. You slid your left hand inside my board shorts and began kneading my bum, stroking it, running your fingers up my crevice and up my back. It was making me wild. I could feel my penis becoming harder by the second until there was no more room in my pants for it to expand. I turned over slightly to give you better access and you immediately ripped the Velcro apart. I felt a sudden release of pressure as my penis instantly became erect. You were so close to it, looking at it, stroking it, yet you resisted my will that would coax you closer still. Your gentle touch was so perfect and it was all I could do to stop me climaxing. Wheelbarrows, South Sydney Rabbito's, Trail Bike Riding, Julia Gillard: I was clutching at straws. Anything to take my mind off how irresistible your touch was.

I peeled off your frock, exposing your shoulders and then your breasts. Your lingerie was intimate; sensual yet adventurous; confident yet vulnerable; a contradiction yet in harmony with the girl I knew. We sat up. I kissed you on the lips and the neck. My hands were wandering. I didn't know where to put them next. You were so beautiful, anywhere would have done, but I wanted you to feel amazing. I wanted it to be perfect for you.

You put your hand on my head and gently pushed down, sending me in the direction of your devil's playground. I placed my hand between your knees and delicately parting them. You were intent on making me work for my pleasure. I moved my hand closer and closer, prising your thighs further apart until I reached my destination. I kissed your left inner thigh lightly and then your right. I placed two of my fingers under the elastic of your lingerie and I slid them back and forth, slowly pulling the undergarment to one side. I took two fingers and parted your lips teasing you. As I got closer, you thrust your pelvis to try and force me into you. As I lightly moved my tongue over you, I could see your love juice glistening from the reflection of the lights over Port Macquarie.

I licked slowly at first; long, slow strokes. Then faster as I reached your clitoris. Faster and faster; a feverish frenzy. I could feel your body going into spasm. You were feeling so much pleasure. You were rubbing your hands through my hair and pushing my tongue further inside you. I slid one finger inside you, then two, three. Your body began to shake. I couldn't stop. The taste of you on my tongue, in my mouth. You were so wet that your love syrup had trickled down onto the warm rock beneath us.

You had your hand curled tenderly around my penis, sliding it up and down. A secretion of semen had started to ooze from my member. You slid your finger over it caressing it into my head and shaft. As I felt my penis start to pulse, I put my hand on your hand to stop you. I could hear you breathing deeply– a coarse raspy gasping breath – and I watched your face as rapturous exhilaration overwhelmed you as you reached the end of your journey.

I turned and plunged my member deep into you. The passion of your lips were upon mine as our hips collided. Over and over I penetrated; deeper and deeper inside you. A small sound escaped your lips; a little squeak, a hint of the pleasure you were feeling. I opened my eyes and I looked at you. Your eyes were closed. I would've given anything to know what was going on inside your head.

I felt warm and I could feel myself building to an apocalyptic eruption. I wanted to go faster but I held back. I slowed because I wanted you to feel me fill you with my cum, while looking deeply into your beautiful eyes. As I started to come, I could feel you react to my penis as it pulsated inside you.

We lay there for what seemed an eternity. I didn't want to leave. After a while, we dressed each other and started on the long walk back along the break-wall. As we walked, our hands were touching and I linked my little finger in yours. For a time, at least, we could continue to be one. We kissed once more and then you turned and walked away. I waited until I saw you disappear into the darkness.

When would our next encounter be? I wondered. I knew it would only be until the next time I sat alone, quietly, and thought of my Jann.

She read it and wrote back immediately. 'That was amazing. Can't talk now. I have to masturbate.' I laughed to myself, knowing that she wasn't joking. A little while later, she wrote, 'Ah, that's better. You are so lucky you're not here right now.'

I wrote back, 'No, Jann, you're the lucky one. One night with me, and you'd never want to leave.'

She replied, 'Mmm, probably right.'

'Tell me, Jann, what is your dream for the future?'

She said, 'Ok. I want no stress, to travel in five-star luxury, and a hot tub to drink champagne in under the stars.'

I said, 'That sounds great.'

She asked, 'What's yours?'

I answered, 'The same as yours but with you.'

'Mmm, perfect. Night,' Jann replied.

She had this funny little habit. At night, when we were chatting, she wouldn't say she was going to sleep. She'd just finish the sentence she was on, write the word 'Night' and that was it.

CHAPTER SEVENTEEN

It was very apparent to me that, given how my online romance with Jann had escalated, something had to give. Here I was married to a woman I love dearly and I was having a non-sexual affair with the woman I considered to be the 'One'. It was funny how I could justify to myself marrying a woman I'm in love with, but constantly think about another woman that I would've liked to spend my life with had Sophie and I never met.

In the beginning, Jann and I had agreed that I wouldn't give her my phone number unless she asked for it. I thought to myself, *Bugger it! What have I got to lose? Besides a marriage, of course.* So the next day I sent it through. Ten minutes later, she texted me her number with four smiley faces. I phoned her straightaway.

The apprehension and anticipation was incredible. When Jann answered the phone, I thought to myself, *Nothing's changed. Her voice sounds exactly as I remember it.*

We started talking, in general at first, but then she said to me, 'You know we have to meet, don't you?'

I replied, 'Yes, I think that's inevitable.'

'You know that'll probably lead to us having sex don't you?' I could hear the smile in her voice.

'Is that a problem for you?'

'No' she said matter of factly.

We discussed the logistics of us meeting. We knew it would be difficult. But, with air travel being more frequent, a day trip up to Brisbane would go relatively unnoticed. An hour up, four hours together, then an hour back. Easy!

It seemed to me that, although Jann was playing along with the fantasy, she was likely to come up with an objection that would throw water on the fire, but I wouldn't let her. I had an answer for everything. There was one thing I was fairly certain of though, and that was that, deep down, I really didn't think we were ever going to meet. Nevertheless, we made plans.

I watered down the reason for a meeting from having sex to sitting somewhere together for a cup of tea and a chat. When I thought about it, for me it wasn't really about the sex. It was more about the emotional connection. In the end, I just wanted to see my Jann again.

She told me that Ashley had to go a conference in Sydney and that we could meet for lunch. I thought, *What a great idea. Then I wouldn't have to explain to Sophie what I was doing in Brisbane if the return flight got cancelled.*

I could tell from Jann's voice that she was nervous. Trust was a big issue with her husband. I changed the subject for a little while and we spoke about other things. I looked at my watch and noticed that we had been on the phone for an hour and a half. I was never going to hang up and Jann knew it.

Nearing the end of the conversation, Jann expressed her concerns again, so I said to her, 'Look, Jann, at the end of the day, I would rather be your mate and have you in my life than not have you in my life at all. If this is all too much for you, I will back off. I'll hate it, but I'll do it for you because all I want is for you to be happy.'

She said, 'Mitch, I don't want to be your mate but I'm not sure we can be lovers. I've hurt Ashley before. It nearly killed him and I don't want to do that to him again, but that's where I feel I am heading.'

I said, 'Well, where do we go from here? What's between mates and lovers? We'll just have to be 'somethings'. There you go; we've just created a whole new category of relationship between mates and lovers.'

She said, 'I like it. Let's try being 'somethings'.'

She said she had to go, as Ashley had just arrived home, and so we hung up. I was feeling on top of the world, not because we were going to have a physical affair, but because we had decided that, whatever we were, we would stay in contact, and that was the most important thing to me.

That hour and a half felt like ten minutes. It was the first of many phone calls, and every time we spoke I felt closer to her. *Soon*, I thought, *my distant shadow will become my infrequent lover*. Because of the hesitation she felt though, I knew it wasn't yet a done deal.

CHAPTER EIGHTEEN

After that phone call, I knew I had a decision to make – the hardest decision I would ever make in my life. I decided to tell Sophie what was going on. Boy, was that a mistake!

I got home after work and gave Sophie a kiss. She said, 'What's wrong?'

'We need to talk.'

She said, 'Oh no! What's wrong?'

'After dinner, we'll have a chat,' I said.

Sophie always knew how I was feeling. She always knew when something was wrong. I guess that's why she didn't pick up on anything really, until now because I'd been feeling happy.

We sat down to dinner and I tried to be as normal as I could be, given what I knew was about to come. At that stage, the kids were none the wiser about what was going on. Sophie and I were masters of deception when it came to hiding our emotions from our kids. We always had plenty of issues to deal with on a daily basis. So to explain the reason for Sophie crying, it was simple enough just to put it down to stress. I was a different story. I very rarely cried in front of the kids, so when it all got a bit too much and I broke down, they would worry. I would always use the 'depression' defense and that usually allayed their concerns.

After dinner, Sophie was finding things to do. I supposed she could sense the enormity of what I wanted to tell her, just not the content. I took her by the hand and said, 'Let's go into our room.' I could see the look of intense worry on her face.

We went in and I shut the door. I said, 'Sit down, I'm about to upset you a bit.'

She said, 'Oh, no!'

I said, 'I need you to not interrupt me because I need to get it out and tell you exactly what's going on.' She didn't say anything so I continued. 'You know I've been emailing Jann … well, it's gone a bit further than I thought it would. Jann is the first girl I ever made love to.' My voice was starting to break and my lips were starting to quiver. 'That fact is, I'm in love with her … I've never not loved her.'

I looked at Sophie and she started to cry. She said, 'How long have you been in love with her?'

I said, 'Since the day I met her.'

Sophie pulled her hand away from mine.

Sophie then broke into tears and said, 'You love her so you don't love me. Our whole marriage has been a lie. Is that it? Our whole marriage is a lie?'

She tried to get up and leave, but I took her by the arm and pulled her back and gave her a hug. She tried to free herself, but I wasn't going to let her go until I had finished telling her everything. I told her that, although I'd had these feelings for Jann for so long, it didn't mean that our marriage was a lie. I loved Sophie more than anything and would never intentionally hurt her but, given the current circumstances, I thought she needed to know. I told her that Jann was living in Brisbane and I was here and that there was no way anything was going to happen between us, even though I wanted something to happen.

It wasn't a matter of loving one or the other, it was a matter of: why can't I love two women at the same time? Where's the rule that says you can't love two people at the same time? I don't think love is exclusive, is it? Is it really that clear cut? Can your heart tell you that, once you break up with someone, you are never allowed to love them again? Your head can tell you that, but which one do you believe – your heart or your head? I haven't figured that one out yet. Love isn't like a light bulb. You just can't flick a switch and it will turn off.

After I explained my dilemma to Sophie, I said, 'I must be mental or something. Most guys would forget someone who treated them like shit and move on, but I can't.'

Sophie said, 'So, do you love her?'

I said, 'Yes.'

'Then you can't love me.'

'I do love you. I love you with all my heart.'

She said, 'I don't understand. I've loved you and I've supported you. We've been through a lot together. I've been through a lot. Why aren't I enough for you?'

'I don't know,' I said quietly. 'But it's not about anything you've done or haven't done. It's about my feelings for Jann.'

We lay on the bed for a while as Sophie composed herself. I kept hugging her to give her some sense of comfort. She was sobbing to the point where no more tears would fall. I had hurt the woman I loved more than she had ever deserved. I had betrayed her. I knew in my head that, even though Jann and I had not been physical with each other, we had nonetheless had an affair, and that had crushed Sophie beyond belief.

Sophie and I agreed that we needed to see a marriage counselor in an attempt to save our marriage. Sophie doesn't like talking about her feelings with me, so I thought telling a stranger might help. I also told her that she should talk to whoever she felt she needed to. She told me she wanted to talk to her friend Carol, but I was unsure about it because her husband, Pedro, and I are good mates.

We had a couple's session with the counselor and then each had a session alone with her. Sophie's level of emotional distress was very high. The counselor told us that there were no right or wrong answers to her questions … just answers. After the combined session and then my single session, I didn't see that as being the case. I was the bad guy here and it was up to me to fix it. I did the only thing I could think of to make her feel better. I secretly called Carol and told her I needed to talk to her. She asked why and I told her I couldn't discuss it over the phone.

I walked around to Pedro and Carol's house on a Sunday morning. Pedro was a bit funny about why I wanted to talk to Carol alone without him there. I told him it was personal and not to worry. I wasn't going to run off with his wife.

Carol and I went for a short walk down to the waterfront at Green Point and I told her everything. Carol is one of those straight-shooters. If you don't want to hear what she has to say … don't ask. I didn't tell Carol in an attempt to seek redemption for myself or acceptance for my actions because I knew I wouldn't get it. I told her for the sole purpose of her being there for Sophie if she needed a shoulder to cry on.

Carol told me how she felt and said that if I were married to her, I wouldn't be any longer. It hurt me to hear

The Fallout

it because that was an option Sophie had available to her and it scared the shit out of me. My friend Leonard had had an affair and his wife, Rachelle turfed him out without a moment's hesitation. I always respected her for that, but that was my greatest fear: that I would suffer the same fate. I feared it because, although Sophie would be justified in getting rid of me, I still loved her with all my heart.

After speaking with Carol, I went home and told Sophie that I had told Carol and why. She accepted it and, I think, appreciated that I was trying to help her cope with the situation as best she could.

Over the next couple of weeks, Jann had issues going on within her family which meant that I had to take a back seat for a while. Her youngest daughter was going overseas for twelve months. Her eldest daughter was turning twenty-one and her dad and 'outlaws' were coming to stay for the celebrations.

I knew something was wrong in my heart when her emails became a bit cryptic. It was like she was sending a message in another language. I received an email that sounded as though it was meant for someone else and I had a feeling I knew who it was. Jann knew I didn't like her talking about her life with other men but she couldn't help herself and did it anyway. When I asked her not to do it anymore, the emails stopped coming.

Since reconnecting, we hadn't gone twelve hours without contact. At this point, two days had passed with no communication between us. I was worried something had gone wrong. *Had Ashley found out?* I wondered. *Had she gone cold on me? Had her old flame come back on the scene?* I didn't know but I felt worried.

I was sitting at home one night when I received a Facebook message from her. It read, 'Did you get my message at work?'

I replied, 'No. Send it to my home address.'

She replied, 'Sent. I really want you to read it.' My stomach started to churn. It seemed that, whenever Jann sent me an email, it was bad news.

I went downstairs to the computer and switched it on. I waited impatiently as it booted up. As I opened the email, I read the opening line which I dreaded – another 'Dear Mitch' letter.

I could feel my heart breaking inside my chest. The pain welling up inside me was overwhelming. I read the letter several times to let it sink in. I replied to the letter with all the dignity I could muster. After replying, I went upstairs, made the cup of tea I'd promised Sophie three quarters of an hour before, and gave it to her in the lounge room. By that time, tears were pouring down my face. She asked me what was wrong and I told her not to worry about it. I hurriedly walked to our bedroom and shut the door before our kids could see the state I was in.

Sophie followed me in and I lay on the bed and started sobbing uncontrollably. I couldn't breathe.

Sophie asked again, 'What's wrong? What's happened?'

The answer I gave was actually quite comical, although I didn't think so at the time. 'She's dumped me.'

Sophie asked, 'Who?'

In a quivering voice, I said, 'Jann. She's just sent me an email telling me she can't see me or talk to me anymore.'

'Oh' she said, with a confused tone of relief and disdain.

She sat down beside me but didn't touch me. I recognised that it would be too much to ask for any compassion from her but I was in absolute agony. I hadn't seen this girl for twenty-five years and had only spoken to her five times on the phone since we'd last seen each other.

'I don't understand how you can be this upset,' Sophie said. 'You are married to me. You are supposed to love me. I don't understand.'

I replied, 'I don't understand it either, Darl. She treats me like crap but I can't help it. She's like a magnet. If you knew her, you'd understand.'

She said, 'I don't want to know the bitch.'

I said, 'Don't call her that please. She's not a bitch; she's a lovely lady. I just don't know what to do. She's all I think about. I can't get her out of my head.'

Sophie asked, 'What has she got that I don't have? I mean, what's so great about her? I've seen her; she's not even that attractive.'

I couldn't look at Sophie but I was thinking to myself, *You have always said beauty is what's on the inside. It just so happens that I think Jann is very attractive. She is also very sexy, intelligent, and open. To me, she is perfect.*

After I settled down, Sophie and I lay on our bed and had a chat. A few things she said to me started to make sense. I started to think about it a bit more deeply and realised that, maybe, Jann doesn't treat me this way because she means to. Maybe it is because she can feel herself getting too close to me. It is her coping mechanism to just shut me out which, unfortunately, hurts me.

We went back out to the lounge room and watched a bit more TV. After a while, we decided to go to bed. It was an odd time to think about making love but that's what was on both our minds. It was really nice because, for the first time in a long while, Sophie made an effort to, not just go through the motions, but emotionally connect to me. That is what I need with my partner and I think that is what's been missing in our marriage for a long time. *The only thing now*, I thought, *is for Sophie to want me in her heart; not to have to make an 'effort' to connect.*

CHAPTER NINTEEN

The next day I sent Jann another email to further explain my response. I asked her to remove me as a friend on Facebook and not to contact me again until she was ready to be with me on the same emotional level. I realised that that would just push her away for good and I didn't want that.

I phoned Jann to speak to her about her email. I tried to hold it together and I guess I did a pretty good job because she didn't know I was teary. I explained to her that I wanted to make sure that she was ok and to assure her that I would be fine. Most of all, I wanted to know if she was going to cut me out of her life again or if it would be ok if we stayed friends and chatted every now and again without all the mushy stuff. She expressed concerns about her ability to keep it plutonic, but I really suspected that she was worried about me dragging her back into a forbidden romance that couldn't be realised.

I assured her that, after speaking to my marriage counselor, I had finally realised that the magic silver bullet was actually within me, and that now that I had deciphered my feelings, only I could fix things. I understood that my love for her was based on the memory of what we had. It was short but intense. Jann was my first sexual partner and, for that reason she will always be special to me. However, as far as my love for her goes, it was now a different kind of love; not one that will haunt my daily thoughts forever.

A couple of weeks later, early in September 2013, Jann texted me that she was coming to Sydney with Ashley, as he had a conference to attend. I texted her back asking if we could have lunch together. She agreed. I didn't tell Sophie of my plans because I knew she would not understand and fret about the possibility of me having sex with Jann. This worry was well founded, as not even I knew what would happen when we met.

As I was crossing the Sydney Harbour Bridge, I texted Jann to make sure Ashley had left the QT Hotel. I parked in an underground parking station and walked to the hotel. Jann was waiting out the front. As our eyes met, she smiled. She looked absolutely amazing. I walked up to her and gave her a kiss on the cheek and a hug.

We started to walk and kept looking at each other. It was hard to keep my eyes off her. Here we were, twenty-six years after the last time we saw each other, and the 'One' I'd been dreaming about was beside me. Amazing!

We headed down to Circular Quay and jumped on the Manly Ferry. We didn't stop talking all the way over. We got off the ferry and walked to a beachfront café. I couldn't believe my ears when Jann started talking about the first time she'd had an affair while she and Ashley were in England before they were married. I'd already heard about Ian, the second affair, the one that lasted for sixteen years, but this first one made me a little skeptical about her ability to commit to one man. It also confirmed to me that Jann has an ability to hold onto the men who love her, no matter what.

As we returned to Circular Quay on the ferry, we continued to talk about things we had done in the past, but never anything inappropriate about us. I had made a booking at Aria at Circular Quay for lunch. It's a very exclusive restaurant and a nice atmosphere for a couple to share lunch and a chat.

As soon as we sat down, Jann started to talk about things that only people who trust each other talk about: her affairs, her husband's premature ejaculation problem, and the fact that she uses sex toys to pleasure herself whenever she needs to. Not that there's anything wrong with that. It kind of turned me on. But, at lunch?

Then out of the blue, she leant across and kissed me. This was no ordinary kiss. It was sensual. It was lovely.

For a while, we sat together eating our lunch. We talked a lot but all I could think about was that kiss. There was a beautiful view on the other side of the glass, but all I could do was look into Jann's eyes. There was one thing that I needed to ask her. In my mind, everything else paled into insignificance. I needed to know what happened twenty-seven years ago. I needed to know why I wasn't good enough for her. It was a question I needed to ask her in order to find a satisfactory response that would give me closure. Then I would finally be able to move on.

Jann's response wasn't what I had hoped to hear. I don't exactly know what would have been an acceptable answer, but this wasn't it. She simply said, 'I don't know. I was pissed most of the time I was at uni. I just wanted to have a good time.'

Things went quiet after that. There was an uncomfortable silence; one I had never experienced with Jann before. Conversation had always flowed easily between us. We sat quietly and ate lunch and drank red wine. It was at this time that I did take in the view of Sydney Harbour and the bridge while I attempted to comprehend what she'd told me and what my response would be.

I had no response. All I could glean from her answer was that, all those years ago, I was her play-toy ... and possibly still was.

It was getting late, so after lunch we started to walk back toward Jann's hotel. It was chilly in the shade of the tall buildings so I put my arm around her. I slid my hand under her blouse so I could feel her skin. It was soft and warm. She put her hand on mine and squeezed it. My head was spinning. I wasn't thinking straight. I had no idea what I was doing.

We were at a pedestrian crossing and she turned to me, so I kissed her.

She said, 'I'd better walk you to your car.'

I didn't say anything. We became silent. There was an anticipation within me that something was about to happen. Did I want it to happen? I didn't know. All I knew was that I wasn't going to make the first move.

We got to the parking station and we walked down to the second level to where my car was parked. I was expecting her to give me another kiss and wave goodbye. Instead, when I unlocked the car, Jann went to the passenger side and got in and waited for me. I got in and I could feel the tension between us. This time when we kissed, it was raw. I put my hand on her breast and she pressed it hard with her hand. With the other hand, I unclipped her bra so I could feel the fullness of her breast within my hand. It was just as I had remembered it.

It was at that moment that I realised what was at stake. I recognised that I had a woman waiting for me at home who loved me deeply and unconditionally. Not just my wife, but my whole family trusted me.

I pulled away from Jann. She tried to pull me closer to her.

I said, 'No Jann, I can't go through with it.'

She leaned over to kiss me again but I said 'No'. She had a look of understanding yet her face conveyed disappointment. She looked so good and it would have been so easy to go all the way. I had never seen a look of rejection on Jann's face before. It was quite upsetting.

The one thing about Jann is that she could always justify within herself that what she was doing was ok. I couldn't. There was absolutely no justification for my behaviour. What I was doing was immoral; just plain wrong. I had no intention of treating my wife and family the same way Jann had treated hers. I never meant to do that and I felt like shit for letting things go as far as they had.

Jann did her bra and blouse up and we sat there for a moment, looking everywhere but at each other. There's not a whole lot of interesting stuff to look at in a parking station.

Finally, I asked her if she was ok. She nodded.

I started the car and drove her up to her hotel. As I pulled up at the front of the hotel she put her hand on my cheek and said, 'We'll talk soon, ok?'

I smiled at her. She opened the car door and was gone, disappearing into the crowd. She didn't look back. That worried me.

I drove off and headed home. As I headed up the F3 Freeway, I received a text message. It was a picture of Jann having a bath in her hotel room. She certainly knows how to tease a guy.

That September day was a day that I won't easily forget. I was happy with my decision not to take things further that day.

Several weeks went by before the topic of that day in Sydney was raised. It was me who raised it. Jann was adamant that we could never meet again because she was frightened by the total loss of control she had felt when she was with me that day. She told me that, when she first saw me, she thought I was gorgeous. She said she didn't think that if we ever met again she could control herself. I did and said everything I possibly could to try to convince her that it was ok. She couldn't see how it would work.

Over the next month or so, we kept lines of communication open. We just talked about everyday stuff. Her daughter had an interview to get into medicine at university. She was very proud of her and I was happy for her too. All sorts of things came up that Jann wanted to share with me. She was very upset one night, telling me how her husband had made her so scared that she'd picked up a knife and fled the house. I was there for her and calmed her down to a point where she returned home. I knew Ashley loved Jann. He would never hurt her. I was confident of that.

I then became aware that Jann's daughter, who was over in England for a twelve-month working holiday, was very ill and that Jann was flying out the very next day. I sent several messages of comfort to let Jann know I was there for her. She replied to them but her replies were getting shorter and more cryptic. I could see the pattern emerging again. I didn't like it when she got like this. I started to prepare myself for another 'break-up'.

Sure enough, I received the final 'Dear Mitch' letter from Jann.

Funnily enough, I wasn't that upset; not as upset as I thought I'd be. But I was angry. A few emails and text messages flowed back and forth before I asked her not to reply to any of my communications. I knew I wasn't strong enough to keep from replying to her emails, so I needed her to be the strong one. I asked simply that she just let me go so that I could do the same and get on with my life.

Before Jann let me go, she hit me with a broadside of insults and untruths about my mannerisms and personality that she didn't like and, in fact, hated. I couldn't believe what I was reading. I was ready to surrender a very important person: one who had been in my life forever, only to be cut down once again. She then stopped answering my emails and texts when I attempted to obtain an explanation for the things she wrote. She had launched into a tirade that was so upsetting to me, I didn't know what do.

I knew from the content of her emails that she was in emotional trouble so I took the drastic step of phoning Ashley, asking him to contact her immediately to make sure she was ok. Because I was so angry and confused, I also told him what was going on with Jann and me. He didn't answer the phone, so I left a message and sent him a text message. After I did that, I sent Jann a text to tell her what I'd done.

Jann replied with, 'You Did What?'

I texted back, 'You forced my hand. You sounded distressed and you wouldn't take my calls, so I had to find out if you were ok.' It was at that moment in time where I knew I'd really stuffed up … badly.

She replied, 'You are a terrible human being, Mitch. You have just ruined my life. I am never ever going to speak to you again as long as I live. Goodbye.'

I also told my wife what I had done. Sophie couldn't believe I would do such a thing. She sided with Jann on the issue. Sophie told me that, if their marriage ended, it would be my fault. I couldn't believe what I was hearing until it finally dawned on me what I had done.

I left another message on Ashley's answering machine explaining that I had made the whole thing up to piss Jann off. I thought that may have bought Jann a bit of credibility but, given Jann's history of having affairs, I don't think it's likely that he would have bought it. The information I left in the first message was so detailed that I think he would have been in no doubt as to the authenticity of my claims.

One of the hardest things I've ever had to do was let go of the person I had fought so hard to keep; the person I have loved since the first day we met in that Sydney bar many years ago. I have tried to contact Jann again since the ill-fated message to Ashley. However, true to her word, she has not contacted me in any way, shape, or form.

I understand fully. It was a terrible thing that I did, letting her husband know about us. It wasn't my place to tell him anything. At the time, I was hurt and angry, as well as concerned. Even though I knew Jann and I were done and would never be in contact again, I still needed to know she was ok. But now I will never know and that is my punishment for what I did.

As passionate and lustful as our cyber-encounter had become, we only met again that one time. It was a meeting of fire and passion but I know it will never happen again. I know we will never speak again either. The hurt Jann has caused me and I have caused to myself will not allow me to think of her the way I used to.

I have learnt that when we continue to let someone in our lives repeatedly hurt us, we are saying to them that they matter more to us than our self-respect and our dignity. And even if they continue with these types of behaviours, we'll still continue to let them in our lives. In order to take a stand for ourselves, we must be willing to part company with people whom we know we've given a significant number of chances to. Though letting go will probably cause us a lot of pain, it's necessary for us to provide the best possible future for ourselves. We have to love ourselves or no one else will.

Seven months passed and I sent Jann a happy birthday message … no reply. She is far stronger than I. The times I think of Jann are now fewer and further between. I no longer harbour the deep-seated passion and lust that I once held for her. I simply remember her in the context of life and past lovers. She will always be a loving memory and she will always be Jann … my distant shadow.

POSTSCRIPT

I still think of Jann. I don't obsess over her anymore, but I like to think that, one day, in the far-off, distant future she will forgive me. I see her on Facebook but control my urge to message her. When I'm in Brisbane, I get that 'so near, yet, so far' feeling, but I have learned to respect her wish for me to leave her in peace.

I haven't heard from Jann since ending our relationship. I don't know if she is ok. I hope she is, because one thing that has never changed is the way I feel about her. I am happy if Jann is happy.

I just hope Jann is content to be living her life the way she is. She told me once how much she loves Ashley and how she could never love another man as much. I hope she sees that, to achieve long-term happiness in their relationship, she needs to commit herself to him 100 per cent. Jann is very insecure within herself, although very at ease with men. However, in my opinion, in order to be truly happy she needs to learn to like herself.

I have ceased my employment at Long Jetty and I still suffer from post-traumatic stress disorder and the depression that goes with it. It is debilitating and I don't ever think you get over it as a sufferer; however, I get on with my life. There is nothing else for me to do but get on with it.

Special mention must go to my family – my wife and three kids. I owe them a debt of gratitude for their support; support that has been undeserved, but appreciated.

I am still married to the same woman who has stuck with me through thick and thin, ups and downs, highs and lows. My wife had every reason to leave me but she didn't. I have only just realised the depth of her love for me. I know the love I have for her has never been in doubt. I love her with all my heart and will do forever. A big thank you must go to her for being a very special lady; one who has more courage, dignity, and humility than I could ever hope to possess. My Sophie.

We have started to communicate a lot more since all this happened, which I think is the key to any good relationship. Since telling Sophie of my 'break-up' with Jann, I have noticed that she looks better and she is carrying herself more positively, as if a big load has been lifted from her shoulders. I think Sophie thought she was at risk of losing me to Jann. Although I would like to think that I was man enough to say unequivocally, 'NO, that would never have happened', I can't. I've always said, 'You can't help who you love'.

If we all lived in a parallel world, we could see where the other path would lead us. We could travel one path with an alternative path always there, just in case we don't like where our chosen path leads us. It's our decision which path we take. Whichever path we do take, we will never know what the outcome would have been had we taken the alternative. That is the mystery of life. Which path to take? What outcome do I want? I have made my decision based on what happened twenty-five years earlier. I met Sophie and promised to love her without question.

Postscript

Sophie puts far more into our relationship than she gets out of it. This isn't how it's supposed to be, I know. I have a lot of work to do. The rebuilding of our relationship continues; the relationship that I almost destroyed. Although I believe that Sophie questioned my love for her, I don't believe that she ever questioned her love for me. I certainly haven't. How lucky am I to have the love of a woman like my Sophie. I love you my darling heart and I look forward to the many memories we will make together in the future.

Our kids are now twenty-three, twenty-one, and eighteen.

From the age of twelve, Annie was a junior representative netball player. In her HSC, she attained an ATAR of 94.6, and gained entry to Sydney University to study Exercise Physiology. During her university course, she studied externally to become a qualified personal trainer. She has also competed in, and finished, the Sydney Half and Full Marathons. She graduated from Sydney University at the end of 2013.

At one stage, Annie also took up rowing. We both loved that sport and I became president of the rowing club. However, I'm glad she gave it up to continue her studies as the 4.00 am starts were killing me. She recently completed a 100 kilometre trail walk for Oxfam, which she and three of her friends completed in thirty-two hours – the same time it took me to drive from the Cairns to the Central Coast in a truck.

Annie took a position as an exercise physiologist in Queensland in early 2014 and moved out of home. It was a very sad time for me because, although we clash about our differing views on life, she is my daughter and I love her deeply. I bought her a new car just to make me feel better. At least I know that she will have a reliable car to drive ... at last. She loves her work and is enjoying being independent. The best part of this electronic age is that communication is never a problem. I can always contact Annie whenever I feel the need for an electronic hug.

Siion is the sanest of any of the females in our family, including my sisters. She is a wonderful shining light who reminds me a lot of Missy. She brightens any room she enters with her happy-go-lucky personality. She is also attractive and smart. She is now in a relationship with a man from Brisbane who is currently living with us; a very nice fella whom I hope will make an honest woman of her one day. She is studying to be a high school teacher at the University of Newcastle and is doing very well, consistently gaining high grades. She is due to graduate at the end of 2015. I love her dearly.

Matt has turned out to be an extremely good looking young fella with a very laid-back attitude to life. I wasn't too bad looking when I was younger either, then something happened. I hope the same thing doesn't happen to Matt. He is smart, is doing very well at school, and is currently studying for his HSC. He is very sports-orientated, gaining a representative place in soccer. He doesn't know what he wants to do with his life but I'm sure he will succeed at his chosen profession. He and I have dirt bikes and ride together as often as we can. He is more or less my best mate rather than my son. I think that all the time Matt and I have spent together is part of the reason we've become mates as well as father and son. That, along with the family values I hold dear, have made him into a fine young man who will succeed in life. He is my second hero. He makes me watch what I do around him. He's my conscience.

My family is my life.

I have lost contact with most of the people mentioned in this book. Some of them with glee, and others, well, they have just drifted away into their own lives or passed away.

The conversation I had on the phone with Missy the week before my final police exams was the last one I ever had with her. I understand that, once Missy and Jann graduated from university, they went their separate ways and lost touch with each other. I'm sorry we parted under these circumstances. I liked Missy a lot. She was a fun person to be around.

Leonard married Rachelle and they had three boys together. They ended their marriage and Leonard moved to Gloucester with another woman, whom he later married. He is the manager of a dairy farm and also raises beef cattle. Rachelle moved back to Taree with the three kids, and is currently in a new relationship.

Clint and his girlfriend, Rose, got married and now live in Narellan with their only daughter and grandson.

The last time we saw Don was at his fiftieth birthday party. About fourteen years had passed since our wedding and I'd seen Don a couple of times when I had to go back to Walgett for court appearances. On our return from our last holiday to New Zealand, there was a letter in the post advising us that Don had passed away. It was a shock and a very sad time for Sophie and me as I considered him to be, not only a great friend, but a mentor. He was a poet, a writer, gained his teaching degree, and opened a café in Walgett to help train the unemployed youth in hospitality.

He was a true humanitarian. He is sadly missed and will never be forgotten.

In later years, Keith lost his way in life. He lost his business, then his wife and kids, and I think, to a certain extent, even his family, although I don't think you ever really lose family. Keith, my childhood hero, died alone on 9 March 2009, aged fifty-two. He is missed. Rheina has moved to Queensland to open her own medical practice.

Sasha and I had a falling out many years ago and haven't spoken much since, apart from the odd hello at a family function. Things between us will never be the same. There has been too much water under the bridge and, although one day I may learn to like her again, I will never get back the sister I once adored. We are both too stubborn to admit defeat in an argument of which I do not even remember the content. We do have semi-regular Facebook contact, but that's not really the same ... is it?

Sasha had left her husband who is an ex-cop. However, I have recently heard that she and her ex-husband are back together. Unfortunately, he has insulted me one too many times, and even I have a point at which I won't take anymore. At Christmas, they have resorted to trickery to get me to attend family functions. I admit, I can be caught once but I won't be caught twice. My nephew Brock has joined the army and is enjoying life.

My brother had his fiftieth birthday recently and the family, minus one insignificant member – my eldest sister– were present. Everything went ok. As expected, Sasha and I got on ok, but it was not like it used to be. We both have our flaws. Oh, how we both have our flaws; but neither worse than the other.

This book is also dedicated to the many people who may, or may not, have appeared in these pages, but who have had an impact on my life. They are the people with whom I have enjoyed different stages of my life and who continue to be an important part of my growth as a human being. If they don't feature in this book that does not mean they are any less important to me. They are loved just the same, and I would like to thank them from the depths of my soul for being a part of my life.

All of these people have played a very important part in my life. They have helped shape me into the man I am today. But there is one person who will stick with me for the rest of my life, forever haunting the deepest recesses of my subconscious … Jann.

www.ingramcontent.com/pod-product-compliance
Lightning Source LLC
Chambersburg PA
CBHW070644160426
43194CB00009B/1569